Soups

BLOOMSBURY KITCHEN LIBRARY

Soups

Bloomsbury Books
London

This edition published 1994 by Bloomsbury Books,
an imprint of The Godfrey Cave Group,
42 Bloomsbury Street, London, WC1B 3QJ.

ISBN 1 85471 517 8

Printed and bound in Great Britain.

Contents

Caramelized Shallot Soup 7
Black Bean, Bourbon and Bacon Soup 8
Sweet Potato and Vegetable Soup 9
Bread Soup 10
Mushroom Soup with Sherry 11
Dilly Avocado Soup 12
Curried Buttermilk and Courgette Soup 13
Leek, Celery and Gruyère Soup 14
Tomato Purée with Yogurt-Ricotta Stars 15
Spring Onion Soup 16
Tarragon-Courgette Soup 17
Black-Eyed Pea and Spring Greens Soup 18
Beetroot and Parsnip Soup 19
Gazpacho Blanco 20
Cold Curried Vegetable Soup 21
Cold Parsley Soup with Icy Tomato Granita 22
Sweetcorn and Coriander Soup 23
Cabbage and Caraway Soup 24
Hot and Sour Soup 25
Puréed Cauliflower Soup 26
Cauliflower Soup Provençale 27
Curried Yellow Split Pea Soup with Lamb and Mint 28
Caraway-Flavoured Celeriac Soup 29
Batavian Endive Soup with Turnips and Apple 30
Peppery Peanut Soup 31
White Bean Soup Cooked with a Bulb of Garlic 32
Chestnut Soup 32
Gazpacho with Roasted Peppers 34
Roquefort Onion Soup 35
Cream of Carrot Soup with Fresh Ginger 36
Chilled Curried Cucumber Soup 37
Turnip Soup 38

Beef and Pasta Soup with Spring Onions and Red Pepper 39
Chicken Soup with Carrots, Potatoes and Spinach 40
Duck Soup with Chicory and Caramelized Pears 41
Veal and Noodle Soup with Sage 42
Sake-Simmered Velvet Chicken Soup 43
Lamb and Wild Rice Soup 44
Chicken, Aubergine and Tomato Soup 45
Chicken Soup with Chilies, Cabbage and Rice 46
Beef Soup with Brussels Sprouts and Sweet Potato 47
Pork Soup with Chinese Cabbage 48
Turkey-Lentil Soup 49
Lamb Broth with Winter Vegetables 50
Vegetable Soup with Grilled Chicken 51
Turkey Goulash Soup 52
Onion and Red Potato Soup with Walnut Toasts 53
Beef and Wild Mushroom Soup 54
Cream of Chicken Soup 55
Oyster Soup with Leeks 56
Crab, Fennel and Tomato Soup 57
Haddock and Sweet Pepper Soup 58
Oyster Soup with Watercress and Carrot 59
Clam and Rice Soup 60
Spinach and Fish Soup 61
Shanghai Scallop Soup with 20 Garlic Cloves 62
Chilled Tomato and Prawn Soup 63
Hot and Sweet Soup with Seafood Dumplings 64
Fish Soup with Red Pepper Sauce 65
Sweetcorn, Scallop and Fettuccine Soup 66
A Fine Kettle of Fish 67
Vietnamese Crab and Asparagus Soup 68
Gingery Pear Soup 69
Golden Gazpacho 70
Peach Soup Flambé 71

Caramelized Shallot Soup

Serves 4
as a first
course

Working
time: about
45 minutes

Total time:
about
1 hour

Calories
190
Protein
4g
Cholesterol
10mg
Total fat
7g
Saturated fat
2g
Sodium
245mg

15 g	unsalted butter	**½ oz**
1 tbsp	safflower oil	**1 tbsp**
500 g	shallots, peeled and thinly sliced	**1 lb**
¼ tsp	salt	**¼ tsp**
	freshly ground black pepper	
12.5 cl	dry vermouth or dry white wine	**4 fl oz**

4 tbsp	balsamic vinegar, or 3 tbsp red wine vinegar mixed with 1 tsp honey	**4 tbsp**
2	garlic cloves, finely chopped	**2**
1 litre	unsalted veal stock, reduced to 60 cl (1 pint)	**1¾ pints**
1 tbsp	chopped fresh mint	**1 tbsp**

Heat the butter and oil together in a large, heavy saucepan over medium heat. Add the shallots, salt and some pepper. Cook the shallots, scraping the bottom of the pan often to prevent the shallots from burning, until they are caramelized – about 30 minutes.

Add the vermouth or white wine, the balsamic vinegar or wine vinegar and honey, and the garlic; cook for 2 minutes, scraping up the caramelized bits from the bottom of the pan. Pour in the stock and bring the liquid to a simmer. Reduce the heat and simmer the soup for 15 minutes. Stir in the mint before serving.

Black Bean, Bourbon and Bacon Soup

Serves 6

Working time: about 1 hour and 30 minutes

Total time: about 3 hours (includes soaking)

Calories 365

Protein 24g

Cholesterol 15mg

Total fat 5g

Saturated fat 1g

Sodium 215mg

500 g	dried black beans, picked over	**1 lb**
500 g	smoked bacon knuckle or forehocks	**1 lb**
500 g	onion, chopped	**1 lb**
5	garlic cloves, chopped	**5**
1½ tsp	dried thyme	**1½ tsp**
¼ tsp	ground cumin	**¼ tsp**

	freshly ground black pepper	
3 tbsp	soured cream	**3 tbsp**
6 tbsp	plain low-fat yogurt	**6 tbsp**
1	spring onion, trimmed and finely chopped	**1**
4 tbsp	bourbon	**4 tbsp**

Rinse the beans, then put them into a large saucepan and pour in enough cold water to cover them by about 7.5 cm (3 inches). Discard any beans that float to the surface. Cover the pan, leaving the lid ajar, and slowly bring the liquid to the boil over medium-low heat. Boil the beans for 2 minutes, then turn off the heat and soak the beans, covered, for at least 1 hour.

Place the bacon in a large, heavy saucepan. Pour in 3.5 litres (5½ pints) of water and bring it to the boil. Cook the bacon over high heat for 20 minutes, skimming off any impurities.

Drain the beans and add them to the pan. Return the mixture to the boil and cook it for 15 minutes more, stirring and skimming from time to time.

Reduce the heat to medium. Add the onion,

garlic, thyme, cumin and some freshly ground pepper. Simmer the soup, stirring occasionally and skimming any foam from the surface, until the beans are tender – 1½ to 2 hours.

While the beans are cooking, whisk together the soured cream, yogurt and chopped spring onion; set the mixture aside.

When the beans finish cooking, remove the soup from the heat. With tongs or a slotted spoon, take out the bacon and set aside to cool. When the bacon is cool enough to handle, separate the meat from the skin and bones by hand. Cut the meat into small pieces and return it to the soup.

Whisk in the bourbon and bring to the boil. Remove from the heat and garnish each portion with a dollop of the soured-cream-yogurt mixture.

Sweet Potato and Vegetable Soup

Serves 6
as a first
course

Working
time: about
45 minutes

Total time:
about
2 hours

Calories
95

Protein
4g

Cholesterol
0mg

Total fat
1g

Saturated fat
0g

Sodium
105mg

2	large sweet potatoes (about 500 g/ 1 lb), scrubbed	2	
600 g	cauliflower, cored and cut into florets, core and leaves reserved	1¼ lb	
3	onions (about 500 g/1 lb), 2 thinly sliced, the other cut into small chunks	3	
1	whole garlic bulb, halved horizontally	1	

250 g	courgettes, scrubbed, trimmed and cut into 2 cm (¾ inch) rounds	8 oz	
1	lemon, juice only	1	
	freshly ground black pepper		
1 tbsp	fresh thyme, or ¾ tsp dried thyme	1 tbsp	
1 tsp	whole cloves	1 tsp	
½ tsp	ground allspice	½ tsp	
¼ tsp	salt	¼ tsp	

Bake one of the sweet potatoes in a preheated 190°C (375°F or Mark 5) oven until it is quite soft – 50 minutes to 1 hour. When the sweet potato is cool enough to handle, peel it and set it aside.

Meanwhile, peel the remaining sweet potato and cut it crosswise into thin slices. Set the slices aside. Cut the cauliflower core into chunks and set the chunks aside with the leaves.

Put the onion slices, cauliflower chunks and leaves (but not the florets), raw potato slices, garlic, lemon juice and some pepper in a large, non-reactive pan. Pour in 2 litres (3½ pints) of water and bring to the boil. Reduce the heat and simmer the mixture; skim off any impurities that have collected on the surface. Add the thyme and cloves, and simmer the liquid until it is reduced by half – about 40 minutes.

Strain the liquid through a fine sieve into a bowl, pushing down on the vegetables with a wooden spoon to extract all their juices. Return the strained liquid to the pan; discard the solids.

Purée the baked sweet potato in a food processor or blender along with 12.5 cl (4 fl oz) of the strained liquid. Whisk the purée into the liquid in the pan. Add the onion chunks, cauliflower florets, allspice, salt and pepper. Bring the liquid to a simmer and cook it for 5 minutes. Add the courgette rounds and cook the soup until the courgettes are tender. Serve hot or cold.

Bread Soup

Serves 4

Working
time: about
35 minutes

Total time:
about
1 hour

Calories
275

Protein
10g

Cholesterol
6mg

Total fat
11g

Saturated fat
2g

Sodium
605mg

45 g	2.5 cm (1 inch) bread cubes, cut from day-old French bread	**1¼ oz**
2 tbsp	olive oil	**2 tbsp**
1	large leek, trimmed, split, washed thoroughly to remove all grit, and thinly sliced	**1**
2	garlic cloves, finely chopped	**2**
1	small head chicory, trimmed, split lengthwise, and sliced crosswise	**1**
30 g	prosciutto (about 2 thin slices), julienned	**1 oz**
250 g	rocket or fresh kale, washed and stemmed	**8 oz**
1.5 litres	unsalted chicken or veal stock	**2½ pints**
2	potatoes, peeled and sliced	**2**
5	drops Tabasco sauce	**5**
½ tsp	salt	**½ tsp**
¼ tsp	crushed black peppercorns	**¼ tsp**

Preheat the oven to 180°C (350°F or Mark 4). Arrange the bread cubes in a single layer on a baking sheet and bake them until they are toasted – about 15 minutes.

Heat the oil in a large, heavy-bottomed saucepan over medium heat. Add the leek and cook it, stirring frequently, until it begins to brown – about 10 minutes. Stir in the garlic, chicory and prosciutto, and continue cooking, stirring occasionally, until the chicory softens –

approximately 5 minutes. Add the rocket or kale and cover the pan; cook the mixture until the rocket or kale wilts – about 3 minutes more.

Stir in the stock, potatoes and Tabasco sauce. Reduce the heat, cover the pan and simmer the soup until the potatoes are tender – about 15 minutes.

Stir in the salt, pepper and toasted bread cubes; allow the bread cubes to soak up some of the broth before serving the soup.

Mushroom Soup with Sherry

Serves 4 as a first course

Working (and total) time: about 45 minutes

Calories 140
Protein 5g
Cholesterol 15mg
Total fat 8g
Saturated fat 3g
Sodium 355mg

7 g	unsalted butter	**¼ oz**
½ tbsp	safflower oil	**½ tbsp**
1	onion, thinly sliced	**1**
500 g	mushrooms, wiped clean, trimmed and thinly sliced	**1 lb**
1 litre	unsalted chicken stock	**1¾ pints**
4 tbsp	single cream	**4 tbsp**
4 tbsp	dry sherry	**4 tbsp**
½ tsp	salt	**½ tsp**
	freshly ground black pepper	
1-2 tbsp	chopped fresh parsley	**1-2 tbsp**

Melt the butter with the oil in a large, heavy or non-stick frying pan over medium-high heat. Add the onion and sauté it, stirring often, for 4 minutes. Add the mushrooms, reduce the heat to medium, and cover the pan to help them release their moisture. Cook for 2 minutes, stirring several times.

Uncover the pan and increase the heat to medium high. Sauté the mushrooms and onions, stirring from time to time, until all of the moisture has evaporated – about 10 minutes. Continue sautéing, stirring the mixture frequently to prevent sticking, until the mushrooms and onions are golden-brown all over – 5 to 10 minutes more.

Transfer the mushroom mixture to a large saucepan; add the stock, sherry, salt and some pepper. Simmer the soup for 15 minutes. Stir in the cream and the parsley, and allow the soup to heat through before serving.

The soup is better reheated after a mellowing period in the refrigerator. It will keep refrigerated for as long as three days.

Dilly Avocado Soup

Serves 6

Working time: about 15 minutes

Total time: about 1 hour and 15 minutes (includes chilling)

Calories 110
Protein 5g
Cholesterol 5mg
Total fat 7g
Saturated fat 2g
Sodium 165mg

1	avocado, halved, peeled and cut into chunks, the stone reserved	**1**
½ litre	plain low-fat yogurt	**16 fl oz**
35 cl	unsalted chicken stock	**12 fl oz**
2	spring onions, trimmed and cut into 5 mm (¼ inch) lengths	**2**

1 tbsp	finely cut fresh dill, or ½ tbsp dried dill	**1 tbsp**
¼ tsp	dry mustard	**¼ tsp**
¼ tsp	salt	**¼ tsp**
	dill sprigs for garnish (optional)	

Put the avocado chunks, yogurt, stock, spring onions, dill, mustard and salt in a blender or food processor and purée the mixture until it is completely smooth. Transfer the soup to a non-reactive container (include the avocado stone, if you like – see note opposite) and tightly cover the container. Chill the soup in the refrigerator for at least 1 hour. If you wish, garnish each serving with a small sprig of dill.

Editor's Note: Because avocado darkens when exposed to air, cut it just before you purée the soup. The yogurt will help keep the soup from discolouring as it chills, but you may also want to try the Mexican trick of leaving the avocado stone in the soup until serving time.

Curried Buttermilk and Courgette Soup

Serves 6
as a first
course

Working
time: about
30 minutes

Total time:
about
1 hour

Calories
95
Protein
3g
Cholesterol
2mg
Total fat
5g
Saturated fat
1g
Sodium
260mg

1½ tbsp	safflower oil	1½ tbsp	1	small apple, peeled, cored and sliced	1
1	small onion, chopped	1	¾ litre	unsalted chicken stock	1¼ pints
2	garlic cloves, finely chopped	2	½ tsp	salt	½ tsp
1½ tbsp	finely chopped ginger root	1½ tbsp	1 tbsp	fresh lemon juice	1 tbsp
½ tsp	ground coriander	½ tsp	¼ litre	buttermilk	8 fl oz
½ tsp	ground cumin	½ tsp	1 tbsp	finely cut fresh chives	1 tbsp
½ tsp	turmeric	½ tsp			
750 g	courgettes, thickly sliced	1½ lb			

Heat the oil in a large, heavy-bottomed saucepan over medium-high heat. Add the onion and sauté it, stirring often, until it is translucent – about 5 minutes. Stir in the garlic, ginger, coriander, cumin and turmeric; sauté the mixture, stirring constantly, for 1 minute. Add the courgettes and apple, and cook the mixture for 1 minute more. Pour in the stock and add the salt. Bring the

mixture to the boil, then reduce the heat and simmer the soup, partially covered, for 30 minutes.

Purée the soup in several batches in a blender or food processor. Return the soup to the pan; whisk in the lemon juice and buttermilk. Cook the mixture over medium heat until it is heated through – 2 to 3 minutes. Garnish the soup with the chives before serving.

Leek, Celery and Gruyère Soup

Serves 4
as a first
course

Working
time: about
30 minutes

Total time:
about
1 hour and
15 minutes

Calories
245
Protein
13g
Cholesterol
25mg
Total fat
9g
Saturated fat
5g
Sodium
400mg

1 litre	unsalted chicken stock	1¾ pints
1	leek, trimmed, all but 2.5 cm (1 inch) of the green tops discarded, split, washed thoroughly to remove all grit, and chopped	1
7	sticks celery, chopped, several whole leaves reserved for garnish	7
½ tsp	fresh lemon juice	½ tsp

2	waxy potatoes, peeled and diced	2
¼ tsp	salt	¼ tsp
2	garlic cloves, peeled	2
7-8	drops Tabasco sauce	7-8
¼ tsp	white pepper	¼ tsp
12.5 cl	semi-skimmed milk	4 fl oz
90 g	Gruyère cheese, grated	3 oz

Heat 12.5 cl (4 fl oz) of the stock in a large, heavy-bottomed saucepan over medium heat. Add the leek, chopped celery and lemon juice, and cook the mixture until the leek is translucent – about 5 minutes. Add the potatoes and cook the mixture for 7 minutes more, stirring often. Pour in the remaining stock, then add the salt and bring the liquid to the boil. Reduce the heat; add the garlic cloves and simmer the mixture, partially covered, for 30 minutes.

Purée the soup in a blender, food processor or food mill, and return it to the pan. Add the Tabasco sauce, and bring the soup to a simmer. Remove the pan from the heat and season the soup with the white pepper. Whisk in the milk and half of the cheese, stirring until the cheese is smoothly incorporated – about 2 minutes. Garnish the soup with the remaining cheese and the reserved celery leaves and serve immediately.

Tomato Purée with Yogurt-Ricotta Stars

Serves 6 as a first course
Working time: about 25 minutes
Total time: about 45 minutes

Calories 95
Protein 4g
Cholesterol 5mg
Total fat 4g
Saturated fat 1g
Sodium 155mg

1 tbsp	virgin olive oil	1 tbsp
500 g	onions, chopped	1 lb
1	carrot, thinly sliced	1
1 tsp	fresh thyme, or	1 tsp
	¼ tsp dried thyme	
3	garlic cloves, chopped	3
	freshly ground black pepper	

800 g	canned tomatoes, seeded and coarsely chopped, with their juice	1¾ lb
30 cl	unsalted chicken or vegetable stock	½ pint
¼ tsp	salt	¼ tsp
90 g	low-fat ricotta cheese	3 oz
2 tbsp	plain low-fat yogurt	2 tbsp
60 g	watercress sprigs, stems trimmed	2 oz

Heat the oil in a large, heavy-bottomed saucepan over medium heat. Add the onions, carrot, thyme, garlic and some pepper, and cook the mixture, stirring it often, until the onions are translucent – 7 to 10 minutes. Add the tomatoes and their juice, the stock and the salt. Reduce the heat and simmer for 30 minutes.

While the soup is cooking, purée the cheese and yogurt together in a food processor, blender or food mill. Set the purée aside.

Now purée the soup in batches, processing each batch for about 1 minute. Return the puréed soup to the pan, bring it to a simmer over medium heat and add the watercress. Simmer the soup just long enough to wilt the watercress – about 1 minute – then ladle the soup into warmed serving bowls.

Gently spoon 1 heaped tablespoon of the ricotta-yogurt mixture into the middle of each bowl. With a tip of a knife, make a star pattern by pushing a little of the mixture out from the centre in several directions. Serve the soup at once.

Spring Onion Soup

Serves 8 as a first course

Working time: about 15 minutes

Total time: about 50 minutes

Calories
75
Protein
4g
Cholesterol
2mg
Total fat
3g
Saturated fat
1g
Sodium
150mg

1 tbsp	virgin olive oil	**1 tbsp**
4	bunches spring onions, trimmed, white parts cut into 2.5 cm (1 inch) lengths, green parts sliced into 5 mm (¼ inch) pieces	**4**
2 litres	unsalted chicken stock	**3½ pints**
1	tarragon sprig, leaves stripped and chopped, stem reserved, or 2 tsp dried tarragon	**1**
¼ tsp	salt	**¼ tsp**
	freshly ground black pepper	

In a large, heavy-bottomed saucepan, heat the oil over medium-high heat. Add the white parts of the spring onions and sauté until soft – about 2 minutes. Pour in the stock and add the tarragon stem or 1 teaspoon of dried tarragon, the salt and some pepper. Reduce the heat and cook at a strong simmer, uncovered, for 30 minutes. Remove the tarragon stem, if using.

Add to the pan the tarragon leaves or the remaining teaspoon of dried tarragon, and the green parts of the spring onions. Cook the soup until the spring onion greens are tender – about 4 minutes more.

Tarragon-Courgette Soup

Serves 8
as a first
course

Working
time: about
50 minutes

Total time:
about
1 hour and
10 minutes

Calories
110

Protein
5g

Cholesterol
7mg

Total fat
5g

Saturated fat
2g

Sodium
230mg

15 g	unsalted butter	½ oz	1½ tbsp	finely chopped fresh	1½ tbsp
1 tbsp	safflower oil	1 tbsp		tarragon, plus several	
3	onions, chopped	3		tarragon stems tied in a bundle	
750 g	courgettes, trimmed and cut	1½ lb	¼ litre	semi-skimmed milk	8 fl oz
	into 2.5 cm (1 inch) pieces		½ tsp	salt	½ tsp
2	carrots, thinly sliced	2		freshly ground black pepper	
1.5 litres	unsalted chicken stock	2½ pints		pinch of cayenne pepper	

Melt the butter with the safflower oil in a large, heavy-bottomed saucepan over medium heat. Add the onions and cook them, stirring often, until they are golden – 15 to 20 minutes. Add the courgettes, carrots, chicken stock and tarragon stems, and bring the mixture to the boil. Reduce the heat, cover the pan, and simmer the liquid for 15 minutes. Remove the lid, increase the heat, and boil the soup, skimming off any impurities that rise to the surface. Continue to cook, stirring occasionally, until the soup is reduced by about one third – 20 to 25 minutes.

Remove the pan from the heat and discard the bundle of tarragon stems. Pour the soup into a large bowl. Purée about two thirds of the soup in a blender or food processor. Return the purée to the pan. Briefly process the remaining third of the soup to achieve a coarse consistency, and pour it back into the pan. Stir in the milk, salt, black pepper and cayenne pepper. Reheat the soup gently without letting it come to the boil. Stir in the chopped tarragon. serve the soup either warm or chilled.

Black-Eyed Pea and Spring Greens Soup

Serves 6

Working time: about 45 minutes

Total time: about 2 hours and 30 minutes (includes soaking)

Calories 130
Protein 8g
Cholesterol 5mg
Total fat 5g
Saturated fat 1g
Sodium 500mg

190 g	dried black-eyed peas, picked over	**7 oz**
1 tbsp	safflower oil	**1 tbsp**
125 g	chopped onion	**4 oz**
30 g	mild back bacon, cut into 5 mm (¼ inch) dice	**1 oz**
1	garlic clove, finely chopped	**1**
1	bay leaf	**1**
¼ tsp	crushed hot red pepper flakes	**¼ tsp**
1.25 litres	unsalted brown or chicken stock	**2 pints**
250 g	spring greens, trimmed, washed and coarsely chopped	**8 oz**
1 tsp	salt	**1 tsp**
2 tsp	cider vinegar	**2 tsp**

Rinse the peas under cold running water, then put them into a large, heavy pan and pour in enough cold water to cover them by about 7.5 cm (3 inches). Discard any peas that float to the surface. Cover the pan, leaving the lid ajar, and slowly bring the liquid to the boil over medium-low heat. Boil the peas for 2 minutes, then turn off the heat, cover the pan, and let the peas soak for at least 1 hour. (Alternatively, soak the peas in cold water overnight.)

Heat the oil in a large, heavy-bottomed saucepan over medium heat. Add the onion and sauté it, stirring occasionally, until it is translucent – about 4 minutes. Add the bacon and garlic, and cook them for 2 minutes, stirring frequently.

Drain the peas and add them to the pan along with the bay leaf, red pepper flakes and stock. Bring the liquid to the boil, then reduce the heat to maintain a simmer, and partially cover the pan. Cook the mixture for 40 minutes, stirring gently several times. Toss in the spring greens and the salt, and cook until the greens are soft and the peas are tender – about 10 minutes. Remove and discard the bay leaf. Stir in the vinegar and serve the soup immediately.

Beetroot and Parsnip Soup

Serves 8
as a first
course

Working
time: about
30 minutes

Total time:
about
50 minutes

Calories
120
Protein
3g
Cholesterol
5mg
Total fat
3g
Saturated fat
2g
Sodium
150mg

½ litre	unsalted veal, vegetable or chicken stock	16 fl oz
500 g	beetroots, peeled and coarsely grated	1 lb
250 g	parsnips, peeled and coarsely grated	8 oz
2 tbsp	sugar	2 tbsp
1	large, ripe tomato, skinned and seeded	1
1	apple, peeled, quartered and cored	1

2 tbsp	fresh lemon juice	2 tbsp
2	large onions, finely chopped or grated	2
1 tbsp	red wine vinegar or white wine vinegar	1 tbsp
1 tbsp	finely cut fresh dill, or 1 tsp dried dill	1 tbsp
¼ tsp	salt	¼ tsp
	freshly ground black pepper	
12.5 cl	soured cream for garnish	4 fl oz

Pour the stock and ¾ litre (1¼ pints) of water into a large pan and bring the liquid to the boil. Add the beetroots, parsnips and sugar. Reduce the heat, partially cover the pan and simmer the mixture for 20 minutes.

Purée the tomato and the apple in a food processor or blender, then add the purée to the simmering soup. Add the lemon juice, onions and vinegar. Cover the pan and simmer the soup for 20 minutes more. Stir in the dill, salt and some pepper. Serve the soup piping hot, garnished with the soured cream.

Gazpacho Blanco

Serves 4
as a first
course

Working
time: about
10 minutes

Total time:
about
40 minutes

Calories
165
Protein
7g
Cholesterol
7mg
Total fat
2g
Saturated fat
1g
Sodium
220mg

500 g	seedless white grapes	1 lb	¼ tsp	salt	¼ tsp
2	cucumbers (about 750 g/1½ lb)	2	¼ tsp	white pepper	¼ tsp
1	shallot, sliced	1	½ litre	plain low-fat yogurt	16 fl oz
1	small garlic clove, finely chopped	1	5 to 8	drops Tabasco sauce	5 to 8

Wash and stem the grapes. Cut several of them in half lengthwise and set them aside. Purée the remaining grapes in a food processor or blender. Strain the purée through a sieve and return it to the food processor or blender.

Cut several very thin slices from the centre of one cucumber and set them aside. Peel the cucumbers, halve them lengthwise, and seed them. Cut the cucumbers into thick slices and add them to the grape purée in the processor or

blender. Add the shallot, garlic, salt and pepper, and briefly process the mixture until the cucumbers are reduced to fine pieces.

Pour the mixture into a chilled serving bowl and whisk in the yogurt and Tabasco sauce. Cover the soup and refrigerate it until it is well chilled – about 30 minutes. Serve the soup in chilled bowls, garnished with the reserved cucumber slices and grape halves.

Cold Curried Vegetable Soup

Serves 4 as a first course

Working time: about 20 minutes

Total time: about 2 hours and 20 minutes (includes chilling)

Calories 130

Protein 5g

Cholesterol 1mg

Total fat 4g

Saturated fat 1g

Sodium 220mg

2 tsp	safflower oil	**2 tsp**
1	small onion, thinly sliced	**1**
2 tbsp	mild curry powder	**2 tbsp**
2	garlic cloves, finely chopped	**2**
400 g	canned tomatoes, coarsely chopped, with their juice	**14 oz**
¾ litre	unsalted chicken stock	**1¼ pints**
1 tsp	chopped fresh thyme, or ¼ tsp dried thyme	**1 tsp**
1	sweet green pepper, seeded, deribbed and cut into 1 cm (½ inch) pieces.	**1**

90 g	cauliflower florets, thinly sliced lengthwise	**3 oz**
1	small carrot, thinly sliced	**1**
2	small courgettes (preferably 1 green, 1 yellow), thinly sliced	**2**
1 tbsp	balsamic vinegar or red wine vinegar	**1 tbsp**
¼ tsp	salt	**¼ tsp**
	freshly ground black pepper	

Heat the safflower oil in a large, heavy-bottomed saucepan over medium heat. Add the onion slices and sauté them, stirring, until they are translucent – about 4 minutes. Sprinkle in the curry powder and cook the mixture, stirring constantly, for 1 minute. Add the garlic and cook it for 30 seconds. Stir in the tomatoes with their juice and cook them, stirring frequently, until the liquid is reduced by about one third – 10 to 15 minutes.

While the tomatoes are cooking, pour the stock into a large pot over medium-high heat. Add the thyme and place a steamer in the pot. Arrange the green pepper, cauliflower, carrot and courgettes in the steamer. Cover the pot and steam the vegetables until they are tender – 5 to 7 minutes. Transfer the vegetables to the tomato mixture and pour in the steaming liquid. Add the vinegar, salt and some black pepper, then gently stir the soup to incorporate the vegetables. Refrigerate the soup, partially covered, for at least 2 hours before serving.

Cold Parsley Soup with Icy Tomato Granita

Serves 6
as a first
course

Working
time: about
45 minutes

Total time:
about
3 hours and
45 minutes
(includes
chilling)

Calories
100

Protein
4g

Cholesterol
1mg

Total fat
4g

Saturated fat
1g

Sodium
255mg

1 tbsp	virgin olive oil	1 tbsp
4	spring onions, trimmed and thinly sliced	4
1	onion, thinly sliced	1
2	garlic cloves, finely chopped	2
¼ tsp	salt	¼ tsp
	freshly ground black pepper	
1 litre	unsalted chicken or vegetable stock	1¾ pints
1	potato, peeled and thinly sliced	1

125 g	parsley leaves, preferably flat-leaf	4 oz
6	mint sprigs for garnish	6
	Tomato Granita	
500 g	ripe tomatoes, skinned, cored and quartered	1 lb
¼ tsp	salt	¼ tsp
1 tbsp	fresh lemon juice	1 tbsp
2 tbsp	finely chopped fresh mint	2 tbsp

To prepare the granita, purée the tomatoes in a blender/processor, strain the purée into a bowl. Stir in the salt, lemon juice and mint. Pour into ice-cube trays and freeze it for 2 to 3 hours.

Heat the oil in a large saucepan over medium heat. Add the spring onions, onion, garlic, salt and some pepper. Cook the mixture, stirring often, until the onion is translucent – about 5 minutes. Pour in the stock, add the potato slices. Reduce the heat, cover the pan, and simmer the liquid until a potato slice can be easily crushed with the back of a fork – 25 to 30 minutes.

While the stock is simmering, bring a large

pan of water to the boil. Add the parsley leaves; as soon as the water boils, drain the leaves and refresh them under cold running water.

Purée the parsley and the stock-vegetable mixture together in a blender/processor. Strain the purée into a bowl and let it cool to room temperature. Cover the bowl and refrigerate it until the soup is chilled – at least 2 hours.

Purée the cubes of granita in a food processor until the mixture is grainy. Transfer the soup to 6 chilled bowls. Spoon some of the granita into each bowl; garnish with mint sprigs and serve immediately.

Sweetcorn and Coriander Soup

Serves 4
as a first
course

Working
(and total)
time: about
20 minutes

Calories
160
Protein
5g
Cholesterol
6mg
Total fat
5g
Saturated fat
2g
Sodium
330mg

10 g	unsalted butter	**⅓ oz**	
1 tsp	safflower oil	**1 tsp**	
1	onion, finely chopped	**1**	
3	garlic cloves, finely chopped	**3**	
1 tsp	ground cumin (optional)	**1 tsp**	
1	sweet green pepper, seeded, deribbed and chopped	**1**	
1	sweet red pepper, seeded, deribbed and chopped	**1**	

1	green chili pepper (optional), seeded and finely chopped	**1**	
1	ripe tomato, skinned, seeded, chopped	**1**	
350 g	frozen sweetcorn kernels	**12 oz**	
¼ litre	unsalted chicken stock	**16 fl oz**	
½ tsp	salt	**½ tsp**	
2 tbsp	chopped fresh coriander	**2 tbsp**	

Heat the butter and the oil in a large, heavy-bottomed saucepan over medium heat. Add the onion, garlic and, if using, the cumin. Cook, stirring often, until the onion is translucent – about 5 minutes. Stir in all the peppers and cook them until they soften slightly – about 2 minutes more. Add the tomato, sweetcorn, stock and salt. Reduce the heat and simmer the soup for 5 minutes. Stir in the coriander just before serving.

Cabbage and Caraway Soup

Serves 10
as a first
course

Working
time: about
45 minutes

Total time:
about
1 hour and
45 minutes

Calories
75
Protein
3g
Cholesterol
1mg
Total fat
4g
Saturated fat
0g
Sodium
165mg

2 tbsp	safflower oil	**2 tbsp**
1.5 kg	cabbage, cored, quartered and thinly sliced	**3 lb**
1½ tsp	caraway seeds	**1½ tsp**
1 tsp	mustard seeds	**1 tsp**
½ tsp	salt	**½ tsp**
4 tbsp	red wine vinegar, or white wine vinegar	**4 tbsp**

1 litre	unsalted chicken or veal stock	**1¾ pints**
4	garlic cloves, finely chopped	**4**
400 g	canned tomatoes, puréed with their juice	**14 oz**
¼-½ tsp	cayenne pepper	**¼-½ tsp**
2 tbsp	finely cut fresh dill, or 1 tbsp dried dill	**2 tbsp**

Heat the safflower oil in a large, heavy saucepan over medium heat. Add the cabbage, caraway seeds, mustard seeds and salt. Cover the pan, and cook the cabbage, stirring occasionally, until it is wilted – about 25 minutes.

Add the vinegar and cook the mixture, stirring, for 1 minute. Pour in the stock and ¾ litre (1¼ pints) of cold water, then stir in the garlic, tomato purée and the cayenne pepper. Reduce the heat and slowly bring the liquid to a simmer. Cook the soup gently for 45 minutes. Stir in the dill and serve immediately.

Hot and Sour Soup

Serves 8 as a first course

Working (and total) time: about 30 minutes

Calories 80
Protein 5g
Cholesterol 1mg
Total fat 2g
Saturated fat 0g
Sodium 190mg

1.5 litres	unsalted chicken stock	**2½ pints**
4 tbsp	rice vinegar	**4 tbsp**
2 tbsp	Chinese black vinegar or balsamic vinegar	**2 tbsp**
1–2 tsp	chili paste with garlic, or 5 to 10 drops Tabasco sauce	**1–2 tsp**
1 tbsp	low-sodium soy sauce or shoyu	**1 tbsp**
1 tbsp	dry sherry	**1 tbsp**
½ tsp	finely chopped garlic	**½ tsp**
1–2 tsp	finely chopped fresh ginger root	**1–2 tsp**
1	carrot, julienned	**1**

6	dried shiitake or Chinese black mushrooms, covered with boiling water and soaked for 20 minutes, stemmed, the caps thinly sliced	**6**
15 g	cloud-ear mushrooms (optional), covered with boiling water and soaked for 20 minutes, thinly sliced	**½ oz**
175 g	bamboo shoots (optional), rinsed and julienned	**6 oz**
2 tbsp	cornflour, mixed with 3 tbsp water	**2 tbsp**
250 g	firm tofu (bean curd), cut into thin strips	**8 oz**
1	spring onions, trimmed and sliced diagonally into ovals	**1**

Heat the stock in a large pan over medium-high heat. Add the rice vinegar, Chinese black vinegar, chili paste or Tabasco sauce, soy sauce, sherry, finely chopped garlic and ginger, julienned carrot and sliced shiitake or Chinese black mushrooms, and, if you are using them, the sliced cloud-ear mushrooms and bamboo shoots.

Bring the liquid to the boil, then stir in the cornflour mixture. Reduce the heat and simmer the soup, stirring, until it thickens slightly – 2 to 3 minutes. Gently stir in the tofu. Ladle the soup into the bowls and garnish each serving with the spring onion slices.

Puréed Cauliflower Soup

Serves 8

Working time: about 45 minutes

Total time: about 1 hour

Calories 125
Protein 7g
Cholesterol 15mg
Total fat 6g
Saturated fat 3g
Sodium 230mg

15 g	unsalted butter	**½ oz**
3	onions (about 500 g/1 lb), thinly sliced	**3**
2 tsp	fresh thyme, or ½ tsp dried thyme	**2 tsp**
1 kg	cauliflower, cored, florets cut off	**2 lb**
7	garlic cloves, thinly sliced	**7**

1.5 litres	unsalted chicken stock	**2½ pints**
½ tsp	salt	**½ tsp**
½ tsp	grated nutmeg	**½ tsp**
	freshly ground black pepper	
100 g	low-fat ricotta cheese	**3½ oz**
2 tbsp	plain low-fat yogurt	**2 tbsp**
4 tbsp	single cream	**4 tbsp**
1 tsp	turmeric	**1 tsp**

Melt the butter in a large saucepan over medium heat; then stir in the sliced onions and the thyme. Cover the pan and cook the onions, stirring frequently to keep them from browning, until they become very soft – about 15 minutes.

Reserve 125 g (4 oz) of the smallest cauliflower florets and set them aside for the garnish. Stir the remaining cauliflower florets and the garlic into the onion mixture. Cover the pan and cook the cauliflower for 15 minutes, stirring occasionally to prevent burning. Add the stock, salt, nutmeg and some pepper; simmer the mixture, covered, until the cauliflower is soft – about 20 minutes.

While the cauliflower is cooking, put the cheese and yogurt in a blender/processor, and purée the mixture until it is very smooth. Transfer the mixture to a bowl, then whisk in the cream.

When the cauliflower is soft, purée the mixture in a blender/processor in batches. Return the batches of purée to the pan and keep warm over low heat. Whisk in the cheese-yogurt mixture.

To prepare the garnish, combine the reserved cauliflower florets in a small pan with the turmeric and just enough water to cover the florets. Bring the water to the boil, reduce the heat, and simmer the florets until they are tender – about 7 minutes. Gently place several yellow florets on top of each portion and serve at once.

Cauliflower Soup Provençale

Serves 6 as a first course

Working time: about 15 minutes

Total time: about 40 minutes

Calories 105
Protein 5g
Cholesterol 6mg
Total fat 3g
Saturated fat 1g
Sodium 145mg

750 g	cauliflower, cut into small florets, stems discarded	**1½ lb**
¾ litre	unsalted chicken stock	**1¼ pints**
2	ripe tomatoes, skinned, seeded and chopped	**2**
175 g	onion, chopped	**6 oz**
4	garlic cloves, finely chopped	**4**

1 tsp	dried basil	**1 tsp**
12.5 cl	dry white wine	**4 fl oz**
¼ tsp	salt	**¼ tsp**
	freshly ground black pepper	
2 tbsp	cut fresh dill or chopped fresh basil or flat-leaf parsley	**2 tbsp**
15 g	unsalted butter	**½ oz**

Blanch the cauliflower florets in 2 litres (3½ pints) of boiling water for 1 minute. Drain the florets in a colander and set them aside.

Pour the stock into a large pan. Add the tomatoes, onion, garlic, dried basil, wine, salt and some pepper, and bring the liquid to the boil. Reduce the heat and simmer the mixture for 10 minutes, stirring once.

Add the cauliflower and simmer the soup until the florets are tender – 10 to 15 minutes. Reduce the heat and let the soup simmer for 10 minutes to meld the flavours. Stir in the dill or other fresh herbs and the butter. Serve immediately.

Curried Yellow Split Pea Soup with Lamb and Mint

Serves 4	Calories 325
Working time: about 30 minutes	Protein 20g
	Cholesterol 23mg
Total time: about 2 hours and 30 minutes	Total fat 10g
	Saturated fat 1g
	Sodium 460mg

175 g	dried yellow split peas, picked over and rinsed	6 oz	2	garlic cloves, finely chopped	2
			1	small bay leaf	1
1 tbsp	safflower oil	1 tbsp	2 tbsp	chopped fresh mint	2 tbsp
350 g	lamb shoulder, knuckle end, trimmed of fat	12 oz	1	carrot, thinly sliced	1
			1 tsp	salt	1 tsp
1	onion, coarsely chopped	1	¼ tsp	white pepper	¼ tsp
4 tbsp	thinly sliced celery	4 tbsp	½	lemon, juice only	½
2 tbsp	curry powder	2 tbsp	4	mint sprigs for garnish	4

In a large, heavy-bottomed saucepan, heat the safflower oil over medium-high heat and cook the lamb joint until it is brown all sides – 3 to 5 minutes. Reduce the heat to medium and add the onion, celery and curry powder. Cook the vegetables, stirring constantly, until the onion turns translucent – 3 to 5 minutes. Add the garlic and continue to cook for 30 seconds, stirring to keep the mixture from burning. Add the peas, the bay leaf and 1.5 litres (2½ pints) of water. Bring the mixture to the boil, skim off any impurities, then add the chopped mint. Partially cover the pan, reduce the heat, and simmer the soup until the meat and the peas are tender – about 1 hour.

Remove the lamb joint, and when it is cool enough to handle, trim the meat from the bone; cut the meat into bite-size pieces and set them aside. Remove the bay leaf from the peas and discard it. Purée the peas in a blender or food processor, then return them to the pan. Add the lamb and carrot, and cook, covered, over medium heat until the carrot slices are tender – about 5 minutes. Season the soup with the salt, some pepper and the lemon juice. Serve in individual bowls, each garnished with a sprig of mint.

Caraway-Flavoured Celeriac Soup

Serves 6 as a first course

Working time: about 25 minutes

Total time: about 1 hour

Calories 145
Protein 5g
Cholesterol 7mg
Total fat 7g
Saturated fat 2g
Sodium 315mg

1 tbsp	safflower oil	1 tbsp	
15 g	unsalted butter	½ oz	
2	onions, chopped	2	
750 g	celeriac, peeled and cut into 5 mm (¼ inch) cubes	1¼ lb	
1	carrot, coarsely chopped	1	

2 litres	unsalted chicken stock	3½ pints	
½ tsp	salt	½ tsp	
	freshly ground black pepper		
½ tsp	caraway seeds	½ tsp	
1 tbsp	fresh lemon juice	1 tbsp	
2 tbsp	chopped fresh parsley	2 tbsp	

Put 125 g (4 oz) of the cubed celeriac and ¼ litre (8 fl oz) of the stock into a small saucepan. Bring the mixture to the boil, reduce the heat, and simmer, covered, until the celeriac is tender – about 5 minutes. Set the saucepan aside.

Heat the oil and butter together in a large, heavy-bottomed saucepan over medium heat. Add the onions and cook them, stirring often, until they are translucent – about 10 minutes. Add the remaining celeriac, carrot and 1.5 litres (2½ pints) of the stock, and bring the liquid to the boil. Reduce the heat to medium, cover the pan and simmer the mixture for 15 minutes. Remove

the lid and continue cooking the mixture until it is reduced by one third – about 10 minutes.

Remove the pan from the heat and purée the soup in batches in a blender, food processor or food mill. Return the soup to the pan and pour in the remaining stock along with the reserved celeriac cubes and their cooking liquid. Stir in the salt, pepper, caraway seeds, lemon juice and parsley. Briefly reheat and serve.

Editor's Note: This soup is also excellent served cold with cooked peeled shrimps floating on top.

Batavian Endive Soup with Turnips and Apple

Serves 6
as a first
course

Working
time: about
20 minutes

Total time:
about
50 minutes

Calories
105
Protein
4g
Cholesterol
3mg
Total fat
4g
Saturated fat
1g
Sodium
135mg

1 tbsp	virgin olive oil	1 tbsp
1	onion, chopped	1
2	medium turnips, chopped	2
1	carrot, chopped	1
1 tsp	fresh thyme, or ¼ tsp dried thyme	1 tsp
¼ tsp	salt	¼ tsp
	freshly ground black pepper	
12.5 cl	dry white wine	4 fl oz

1 tbsp	red wine vinegar	1 tbsp
¾ litre	unsalted chicken stock	1¼ pints
1	cooking apple, peeled, cored, chopped	1
350 g	Batavian endive, washed and shredded	12 oz
1	orange, grated rind only	1
4 tbsp	freshly grated Parmesan cheese	4 tbsp

Heat the oil in a large, heavy-bottomed saucepan over medium-high heat. Add the onion, turnips, carrot, thyme, salt and some pepper. Sauté the vegetables, stirring occasionally, until the onion is translucent – about 4 minutes. Pour in the wine and vinegar, and reduce the heat to medium. Cook the vegetables, covered, for 20 minutes.

Pour in the stock and ¾ litre (1¼ pints) of water, then add the chopped apple. Bring the liquid to the boil; then reduce the heat to maintain a simmer, cover the pan, and cook the soup for 5 minutes more. Add the Batavian endive and cook it until it is wilted – about 10 minutes. Sprinkle the orange rind on to the hot soup and serve it immediately with the cheese.

Peppery Peanut Soup

Serves 4

Working
time: about
10 minutes

Total time:
about
25 minutes

Calories
140
Protein
6g
Cholesterol
17mg
Total fat
11g
Saturated fat
4g
Sodium
265mg

10 g	unsalted butter	⅓ oz	¼ tsp	salt	¼ tsp
60 g	celery, finely chopped	2 oz	⅛-¼ tsp	crushed hot red pepper flakes	⅛-¼ tsp
1	garlic clove, finely chopped	1		or cayenne pepper	
1 tbsp	flour	1 tbsp	2	spring onions, trimmed and	2
1 litre	unsalted chicken stock	1¾ pints		sliced diagonally into very	
4 tbsp	single cream	4 tbsp		thin ovals	
2 tbsp	peanut butter	2 tbsp			

Melt the butter in a large, heavy-bottomed saucepan over medium-low heat. Add the celery and the garlic and cook them for 2 minutes. Stir in the flour and cook the mixture for 1 minute, stirring constantly. Whisk in the stock, peanut butter, salt and pepper, and simmer the mixture for 15 minutes. Stir in the spring onions and the cream, and let the soup heat through before serving.

White Bean Soup Cooked with a Bulb of Garlic

Serves 6

Working time: about 45 minutes

Total time: about 3 hours and 20 minutes (includes soaking)

Calories 255
Protein 15g
Cholesterol 1mg
Total fat 5g
Saturated fat 1g
Sodium 465mg

360 g	dried haricot beans, picked over	**12 oz**
1.5 ltrs	unsalted chicken stock	**2½ pts**
1	onion	**1**
1	carrot, halved crosswise	**1**
1	stick celery, halved crosswise	**1**
1	leek, trimmed, split and washed	**1**
1	bay leaf	**1**
2 tsp	fresh thyme, or ½ tsp dried thyme	**2 tsp**

1	whole garlic bulb, skin removed	**1**
1 tsp	salt	**1 tsp**
1 tbsp	virgin olive oil	**1 tbsp**
3	ripe tomatoes, skinned, seeded and chopped	**3**
30 g	fresh parsley, preferably flat-leaf, chopped, plus 1 tbsp for garnish freshly ground black pepper	**1 oz**

Rinse the beans under cold water, put into a large saucepan, cover with water by about 7.5 cm (3 inches). Discard any beans that float to the surface. Cover the pan, leaving the lid ajar, slowly bring the liquid to the boil over medium-low heat. Boil the beans for 2 mins, then turn off the heat and soak, covered, for at least 1 hour.

Drain the beans and return them to the pan. Pour in the stock, add the onion, carrot, celery, leek, bay leaf and thyme. Slowly bring to the boil over medium-low heat. Simmer, and cover the pan. Cook the beans, stirring occasionally and skimming off any foam, until they are tender – 1-1½ hours. Simmer the beans for 30 mins, add the garlic and the salt.

Near the end of cooking, pour the olive oil into a frying pan over high heat. Add the tomatoes and cook for 3 to 5 mins, stirring frequently. Stir in the 30 g (1 oz) of parsley and set the pan aside.

Drain the beans over a bowl. Discard the vegetables except the garlic. Return ⅔ of beans to the pan. Separate the garlic into cloves, and skin. Purée the garlic and remaining beans with a ¼ l (8 fl oz) of the reserved cooking liquid.

Transfer to the pan with the beans and stir in the remaining liquid. Reheat soup over low heat, fold in the tomato mixture. Cook for 1 to 2 mins. Season and serve. Garnish with remaining parsley.

Chestnut Soup

Serves 4

Working time: about 20 minutes

Total time: about 1 hour and 10 minutes

Calories 380
Protein 8g
Cholesterol 6mg
Total fat 9g
Saturated fat 2g
Sodium 220mg

600 g	fresh chestnuts	**1¼ lb**
2 tsp	safflower oil	**2 tsp**
1	leek, trimmed, the green tops discarded, the stalks split, washed, thoroughly and cut into 1 cm (½ inch) pieces	**1**
12.5 cl	dry sherry	**4 fl oz**
125 g	mushrooms, stemmed, caps thinly sliced	**4 oz**
½ to ¾ l	unsalted chicken stock	**¾ to 1¼ pts**
¼ tsp	salt	**¼ tsp**
¼ tsp	white pepper	**¼ tsp**
¼ litre	semi-skimmed milk	**8 fl oz**
1½ tbsp	sliced toasted almonds	**1½ tbsp**

Using a small, sharp knife, cut a shallow cross in the flat side of each chestnut. Drop the chestnuts into 1.5 litres (2½ pints) of boiling water and cook them for 10 minutes. Drain the chestnuts and let them cool slightly; peel them while they are still warm.

Heat the oil in a large, heavy-bottomed saucepan over medium heat. Add the leek pieces and sauté them, stirring frequently, until they are translucent – 4 to 5 minutes. Pour in the sherry, increase the heat to medium high, and cook the mixture until the liquid is reduced by three quarters – 3 to 4 minutes. Add the chestnuts, mushrooms and ½ litre (16 fl oz) of the stock. Bring the liquid to the boil, then reduce the heat and simmer the mixture, covered, until the chestnuts can be easily pierced with the tip of a sharp knife – 25 to 30 minutes.

Purée the mixture in a food processor, blender or food mill. Add the salt and pepper. Pour in the milk in stages, purééing the mixture after each addition. (If you prefer a thinner soup, incorporate another ¼ litre/8 fl oz of stock into the purée.)

Return the puréed soup to the pan and reheat it for 2 to 3 minutes over medium heat. Garnish with the almonds before serving.

Gazpacho with Roasted Peppers

Serves 4
as a first
course

Working
time: about
50 minutes

Total time:
about
1 hour and
50 minutes

Calories
70
Protein
2g
Cholesterol
0mg
Total fat
4g
Saturated fat
1g
Sodium
170mg

1	large sweet red pepper	1
1	large sweet green pepper	1
2	ripe tomatoes, skinned, seeded and coarsely chopped	2
2	sticks celery, thinly sliced	2
1	cucumber, peeled, halved lengthwise, seeded and cut into large chunks	1
2	garlic cloves, chopped	2

90 g	fresh watercress, coarsely chopped, plus 4 whole sprigs for garnish	3 oz
12.5 cl	unsalted veal or vegetable stock	4 fl oz
4 tbsp	fresh orange juice	4 tbsp
1 tbsp	fresh lemon juice	1 tbsp
1 tbsp	virgin olive oil	1 tbsp
¼ tsp	salt	¼ tsp
	freshly ground black pepper	

Preheat the grill. Grill the peppers 5 to 7.5 cm (2 to 3 inches) below the heat source, turning them often, until they are uniformly blistered and blackened – 12 to 15 minutes. Transfer the peppers to a bowl and tightly cover the bowl with plastic film. Let the peppers stand for 5 minutes – the trapped steam will loosen their skins.

Make a slit in one of the peppers and pour the juices that have collected inside it into the bowl. Peel the pepper from top to bottom. Halve the pepper lengthwise, then remove and discard the stem, seeds and ribs. Repeat the procedure with the other pepper.

Put the peppers and their juices into a food processor or blender along with the tomatoes, celery, cucumber, garlic, chopped watercress, stock, orange juice, lemon juice, oil, salt and some pepper. Process the mixture in short bursts until a coarse purée results. Transfer the gazpacho to a bowl; refrigerate it for at least 1 hour, then garnish it with the watercress sprigs and serve.

Editor's Note: This soup may be prepared as much as 24 hours in advance.

Roquefort Onion Soup

**Serves 8
as a first
course**

**Working
time: about
45 minutes**

**Total time:
about
1 hour and
15 minutes**

Calories
200
Protein
7g
Cholesterol
16mg
Total fat
9g
Saturated fat
4g
Sodium
420mg

15 g	unsalted butter	½ oz	2 tsp	fresh thyme, or ½ tsp dried thyme	2 tsp
1 tbsp	safflower oil	1 tbsp			
1 kg	onions, finely sliced	2 lb	2 tsp	fresh lemon juice	2 tsp
2	garlic cloves, finely chopped	2	½ tsp	salt	½ tsp
2 litres	unsalted chicken or veal stock	3½ pints	⅛ tsp	cayenne pepper freshly ground black pepper	⅛ tsp
½ litre	dry white wine	16 fl oz	125 g	Roquefort cheese, crumbled	4 oz
			1 tbsp	chopped fresh parsley	1 tbsp

Melt the butter and oil in a large, heavy-bottomed saucepan over medium-low heat. Add the onions and garlic and partially cover the pan. Cook for 3 minutes, stirring once. Remove the lid and continue cooking, stirring frequently, until the onions are browned – 20 to 35 minutes. Pour in 1.5 litres (2¼ pints) of the stock and the wine, then add the thyme. Bring the liquid to the boil, lower the heat and simmer the mixture until it is reduced by one third – about 30 minutes. With a slotted spoon, remove about

150 g (5 oz) of the onions and set them aside. Purée the soup in a blender, food processor or food mill. Return the soup to the pan and stir in the reserved onions. Pour in the remaining stock, then add the lemon juice, salt, cayenne pepper and some black pepper. Reheat the soup over medium heat for 2 minutes. In the meantime, combine the cheese and parsley in a small bowl and sprinkle the mixture over the soup just before serving.

Cream of Carrot Soup with Fresh Ginger

Serves 8
as a first
course

Working
time: about
30 minutes

Total time:
about
1 hour

Calories
155
Protein
4g
Cholesterol
15mg
Total fat
8g
Saturated fat
3g
Sodium
350mg

1 kg	carrots	2 lb	4 tbsp	sultanas, chopped	4 tbsp
2 tsp	safflower oil	2 tsp	12.5 cl	single cream	4 fl oz
10 g	unsalted butter	⅓ oz	¾ tsp	salt	¾ tsp
275 g	onions, chopped	9 oz		freshly ground black pepper	
4 tbsp	grated fresh ginger root	4 tbsp	2 tbsp	chopped fresh parsley	2 tbsp
2 litres	unsalted chicken stock	3½ pints			

Cut two of the carrots into small dice and set them aside. Slice the remaining carrots into thin rounds.

Heat the oil and butter together in a large, heavy saucepan over medium heat. Add the onions and cook them, stirring occasionally, until they are golden – about 10 minutes. Add the carrot rounds and the ginger, and stir in 35 cl (12 fl oz) of the stock. Reduce the heat, cover the pan, and cook the mixture until the carrots are tender – about 20 minutes.

Pour 1.25 litres (2 pints) of the remaining stock into the pan and bring the liquid to the boil. Reduce the heat, cover the pan, and simmer the stock for 10 minutes. Remove the lid and increase the heat to high. Boil the soup,

skimming the impurities from the surface several times, until the liquid is reduced by about one third and the carrots are soft – 8 to 10 minutes.

While the soup is boiling, bring the remaining stock to a simmer in a small saucepan over medium heat. Add the diced carrots and the sultanas and simmer them, covered, until the carrots are tender – about 5 minutes. Set the saucepan aside.

Purée the soup in batches in a blender, food processor or food mill. Return the soup to the pan over medium heat and add the diced carrots and sultanas with their cooking liquid. Stir in the cream, salt, some pepper, and the parsley. Simmer the soup until it is heated through – about 2 minutes – and serve at once.

Chilled Curried Cucumber Soup

Serves 6 as a first course	Working time: about 20 minutes	Total time: about 1 hour and 20 minutes (includes chilling)	Calories 95 · Protein 5g · Cholesterol 10mg · Total fat 5g · Saturated fat 3g · Sodium 165mg

30 g	fresh coriander, a few leaves reserved for garnish	1 oz
1	onion, quartered	1
2	cucumbers, peeled, quartered lengthwise, seeded and cut into chunks	2
12.5 cl	soured cream	4 fl oz
35 cl	plain low-fat yogurt	12 fl oz
1 tsp	curry powder	1 tsp
¼ tsp	salt	¼ tsp
¼ tsp	white pepper	¼ tsp
3–5	drops Tabasco sauce	3–5
30 cl	unsalted brown or chicken stock	½ pint

Chop the coriander in a food processor. Add the onion and cucumber chunks, and process them until they are finely chopped but not puréed. (Alternatively, you can chop the coriander by hand and grate or finely chop the onion and cucumbers.)

In a bowl, whisk the soured cream with ¼ litre (8 fl oz) of the yogurt, the curry powder, salt, white pepper and Tabasco sauce. Whisk in the cucumber mixture and the stock. Refrigerate the soup for at least 1 hour. Serve the soup in chilled bowls; garnish each portion with a dollop of the remaining yogurt and the reserved coriander leaves.

Editor's Note: This soup is even better when it is made a day in advance.

Turnip Soup

22 g	unsalted butter	¾ oz	¾ litre	unsalted chicken stock	1¼ pints
500 g	small white turnips, peeled, quartered and thinly sliced crosswise	1 lb	3	small waxy potatoes	3
¼ tsp	salt	¼ tsp	2 tbsp	loosely packed fresh chervil leaves or chopped fresh parsley	2 tbsp
¼ tsp	grated nutmeg	¼ tsp			

Melt the butter in a large, heavy saucepan over medium heat. Stir in the turnips and cook them, stirring frequently, until they are golden-brown – approximately 20 minutes.

Season the turnips with the salt and nutmeg, and toss them gently. Remove and reserve 75 g (2½ oz) of the turnips to use as a garnish.

Pour the stock into the pan; then cover it and bring the liquid to the boil. Reduce the heat and simmer the soup for 20 minutes, skimming off any foam that rises to the surface.

At the end of the 20 minutes, peel and quarter the potatoes, then cut them crosswise into thin slices and add them to the soup. Simmer the soup until the potatoes are tender but still intact – 10 to 15 minutes. Taste the soup for seasoning and add more nutmeg if necessary. Garnish the soup with the chervil or parsley and the reserved turnips before serving.

Beef and Pasta with Spring Onions and Red Pepper

Serves 4

Working time: about 30 minutes

Total time: about 1 hour and 30 minutes (includes marinating)

Calories 230
Protein 23g
Cholesterol 40mg
Total fat 7g
Saturated fat 3g
Sodium 445mg

250 g	beef fillet, trimmed of all fat, cut into strips 2.5 cm (1 inch) long	8 oz
1 tbsp	low-sodium soy sauce or shoyu	1 tbsp
1 tbsp	dry sherry	1 tbsp
60 g	capelli d'angelo or other very thin pasta, broken into short lengths	2 oz
2 litres	unsalted brown stock	3½ pints
250 g	Chinese cabbage, cut into 5 mm (¼ inch) wide strips	8 oz

1	sweet red pepper, sliced into very thin strips	1
250 g	firm tofu (bean curd), cut into 1 cm (½ inch) cubes, each cube halved diagonally	8 oz
4	garlic cloves, finely chopped	4
1 tbsp	white vinegar	1 tbsp
3	spring onions, trimmed, green parts only, sliced diagonally into thin ovals	3
	freshly ground black pepper	

Combine the beef strips, soy sauce and sherry in a bowl. Marinate the beef at room temperature for at least 1 hour. Meanwhile, add the capelli d'angelo to 1 litre (1¾ pints) of boiling water with ½ teaspoon of salt. Start testing the pasta after 2 minutes and cook until it is *al dente*. Drain the pasta, rinse it under cold running water to keep it from sticking together, and set it aside.

Bring the stock to the boil in a large pan. Add the Chinese cabbage and cook it for 5 minutes. Stir in the red pepper and cook the mixture until the cabbage and red pepper are tender – about 2 minutes more. Add the tofu, the capelli d'angelo, and the beef and its marinade. Reduce the heat and simmer the soup until the beef is cooked – about 2 minutes. Just before serving, stir in the garlic, vinegar, spring onions and a generous grinding of pepper.

Chicken Soup with Carrots, Potatoes and Spinach

Serves 4

Working time: about 30 minutes

Total time: about 1 hour and 30 minutes

Calories 290
Protein 27g
Cholesterol 70mg
Total fat 6g
Saturated fat 2g
Sodium 430mg

1 kg	chicken, skinned, all visible fat removed	**2 lb**
1	onion, peeled and stuck with 2 cloves	**1**
1	stick celery	**1**
8–12	parsley stems	**8–12**
1	bay leaf	**1**
1 tsp	ground cumin	**1 tsp**
1	sprig fresh thyme, or ¼ tsp dried thyme	**1**
1	whole bulb of garlic, outer papery	**1**

	coating removed, bulb cut in half crosswise	
½ tsp	salt	**½ tsp**
350 g	waxy potatoes, peeled and sliced	**12 oz**
500 g	carrots, sliced into 5 mm (¼ inch) thick rounds	**1 lb**
125 g	fresh spinach, washed, stemmed and sliced into 1 cm (½ inch) wide strips	**4 oz**
	freshly ground black pepper	

Put the chicken into a large pan and add 1.5 litres (2½ pints) of water. Bring to the boil, reduce the heat and simmer for 10 minutes, frequently skimming off the foam. Add the onion, celery, parsley stems, bay leaf, cumin, thyme, garlic and salt, and simmer until the chicken is tender – about 45 minutes.

Drain the contents of the pan into a large bowl. Leave the chicken to cool.

Return the broth to the pan and boil. Add the potatoes, reduce the heat, cover the pan; simmer until the potatoes are tender – about 10 minutes.

Remove the potatoes and set aside.

Add the carrots to the broth, cover, and cook until the carrots are tender – 15 to 20 minutes.

While the carrots are cooking, remove the meat from the chicken into bite-size pieces. Reserve the meat; discard the bones and solids.

When the carrots are cooked, purée half of them with half of the broth in a processor/blender. Transfer to a bowl; then purée the remaining carrots and broth. Pour back into the pan. Add the potatoes, chicken and spinach. Reheat the soup gently and season with pepper.

Duck Soup with Chicory and Caramelized Pears

Serves 6

Working time: about 1 hour

Total time: about 3 hours

Calories 225

Protein 20g

Cholesterol 65mg

Total fat 11g

Saturated fat 5g

Sodium 60mg

2 kg	duck, skinned, meat removed from bones and carcass, trimmed of all fat and cut into 1 cm ($\frac{1}{2}$ inch) cubes; carcass, bones, giblets reserved	**4 lb**
1 tsp	Sichuan peppercorns, toasted and ground	**1 tsp**
1	onion, sliced	**1**
2	slices fresh ginger root, each about 3 mm ($\frac{1}{8}$ inch) thick	**2**

1	small head chicory, sliced	**1**
1 tbsp	safflower oil	**1 tbsp**
2	ripe firm pears, peeled, quartered, cored and cut into thick slices	**2**
2 tsp	sugar	**2 tsp**
2 tbsp	red wine vinegar	**2 tbsp**
3	spring onions, trimmed, green parts sliced, white parts reserved for another use.	**3**

Toss the cubes of duck meat with the peppercorns and refrigerate them while you make the stock.

Chop the duck carcass into 3 or 4 pieces. Put the pieces into a large pan with the other bones and giblets. Set over medium heat and cook for 5 minutes. Pour in water to cover the bones, add onion and ginger. Bring to the boil, skimming any foam. Simmer, for at least 2 hours. Strain it into a large bowl and degrease it.

While the stock is simmering, parboil the chicory. Bring 1 litre (1¾ pints) of water to the boil in a pan over medium-high heat. Add the chicory and cook until tender – about 5 minutes. Drain the chicory and set it aside.

Heat the oil in another large pan over medium heat. Add the cubes of duck and cook, stirring frequently, until browned – about 5 minutes. Remove the cubes and set them aside.

Add pear and cook until translucent but still firm – 5 minutes. Sprinkle sugar over pears, continue cooking, stirring, until the sugar melts. Pour in the vinegar and cook for 2 mins more. Remove the pear and set aside with the duck.

Pour the duck stock into the pan and boil, scraping the pan to dissolve caramelized juices. Add chicory, duck, pears and spring onions to the soup; return it to the boil and serve at once.

Veal and Noodle Soup with Sage

Serves 6

Working time: about 40 minutes

Total time: about 1 hour and 10 minutes

Calories 240

Protein 17g

Cholesterol 75mg

Total fat 7g

Saturated fat 2g

Sodium 385mg

350 g	lean veal, finely chopped or minced	**12 oz**
1	egg, beaten with 1 egg white	**1**
2 tbsp	freshly grated Parmesan or pecorino cheese	**2 tbsp**
2	slices day-old white bread, crumbled	**2**
1	ripe tomato, seeded and finely chopped	**1**
200 g	very finely chopped onion	**7 oz**
1½ tbsp	fresh sage, chopped	**1½ tbsp**
5	garlic cloves, finely chopped	**5**
¼ tsp	salt	**¼ tsp**
	freshly ground black pepper	
1 litre	unsalted veal stock	**1¾ pints**
2	carrots, thinly sliced	**2**
1 tbsp	safflower oil	**1 tbsp**
125 g	capelli d'angelo (angel's hair pasta)	**4 oz**
	fresh sage leaves for garnish (optional)	

In a large bowl, combine the veal, egg mixture, 1 tbsp of the sage, the cheese, bread, tomato, onion, garlic, ¼ tsp of the salt and some pepper. Cover the bowl with plastic film and refrigerate it for 30 minutes. Form the chilled mixture into 18 meatballs, each about 2.5 cm (1 inch) in diameter. Set the meatballs aside.

Pour the stock into a large pan. Add the remaining sage, the carrots, the remaining salt and some pepper. Bring the liquid to a simmer and cook it for about 10 minutes.

While the stock is simmering, pour the oil into a non-stick or heavy frying pan over medium-high heat. Arrange the meatballs in the hot oil, taking care that they do not touch one another. Cook the meatballs on one side until they are well browned – 3 to 5 minutes. Continue to cook the meatballs, turning them frequently, until they are browned on all sides – about 5 to 7 minutes more.

With a slotted spoon, transfer the meatballs to the stock mixture in the pan. Add the pasta and cook it until it is *al dente* – about 4 minutes.

Transfer the soup to individual serving bowls; garnish with the sage leaves if you are using them, and serve immediately.

Sake-Simmered Velvet Chicken Soup

Serves 2

Working time: about 30 minutes

Total time: about 45 minutes

Calories 340

Protein 30g

Cholesterol 70mg

Total fat 6g

Saturated fat 2g

Sodium 320mg

250 g	boneless chicken breast or thigh, skinned, trimmed of all fat and cut into 1 cm (⅓ inch) cubes	**8 oz**	**2**	carrots, sliced into 1 cm (⅓ inch) thick rounds	**2**
1 tbsp	cornflour	**1 tbsp**	**2 or 3**	parsnips, peeled, sliced into 1 cm (⅓ inch) thick rounds	**2 or 3**
60 cl	unsalted chicken stock	**1 pint**	**4**	spring onions, trimmed, sliced diagonally into thin ovals	**4**
4 tbsp	sake or rice wine	**4 tbsp**			
1 tsp	low-sodium soy sauce or shoyu	**1 tsp**			
1–2 tbsp	grated fresh ginger root	**1–2 tbsp**			

Pour 1 litre (1¾ pints) of water into a saucepan and bring it to the boil. Toss the chicken cubes with the cornflour to coat them evenly, then add them to the boiling water; stir with a slotted spoon to separate the cubes. When the water returns to the boil, remove the chicken pieces and set them aside. Discard the water.

Add the stock to the saucepan along with the sake or rice wine, the soy sauce and the ginger. Bring the liquid to the boil, then add the chicken cubes, carrots and parsnips. Reduce the heat to low, cover the pan, and simmer the soup for 15 minutes. Stir the spring onions into the soup 2 minutes before serving.

Lamb and Wild Rice Soup

Serves 6

Working time: about 50 minutes

Total time: about 2 hours

Calories
375

Protein
19g

Cholesterol
1mg

Total fat
13g

Saturated fat
6g

Sodium
275mg

1 tbsp	safflower oil	**1 tbsp**
2	lamb shoulder joints, knuckle end (about 1 kg/2 lb), trimmed of fat	**2**
750 g	onions, coarsely chopped	**1½ lb**
¼ litre	dry white wine	**16 fl oz**
400 g	canned tomatoes, drained and chopped	**14 oz**
¾ litre	unsalted chicken or veal stock	**1¼ pints**
1	carrot, sliced into 5 mm (¼ inch) thick rounds	**1**

8	garlic cloves, chopped	**8**
1	stick celery, chopped	**1**
	freshly ground black pepper	
½ tsp	salt	**½ tsp**
1½ tbsp	fresh rosemary, or 1 tsp dried rosemary	**1½ tbsp**
160 g	wild rice	**5¼ oz**

Heat the oil in a frying pan over medium-high heat. Sauté the lamb until dark brown – about 15 minutes. Transfer the lamb to a saucepan.

Reduce the heat to medium. Add onions and cook, stirring, until browned – 10 to 15 minutes.

Add onions to the pot. Return frying pan to the heat and pour in the wine. With a wooden spoon, scrape up the caramelized juices, stirring to dissolve them. Add the tomatoes and boil until reduced by half. Pour the liquid into the pot, then add the stock, 2.5 litres (4 pints) of water, the carrot, garlic, celery and some pepper.

Place over medium heat and bring to a simmer, skimming. Stir in the salt and rosemary. Simmer until lamb is tender – 1½ to 2 hours.

After 1 hour, put the rice in a pan with ¼ litre (8 fl oz) of water and bring to a simmer over medium heat. Reduce the heat to low and cook until all water is absorbed. Set aside.

Transfer the lamb to a clean surface. When cool enough remove the meat from the bones. Cut into small pieces. Return the meat to the pot. Add the partially cooked rice and simmer until the rice is tender. Serve the soup hot.

Chicken, Aubergine and Tomato Soup

Serves 4

Working (and total) time: about 1 hour

Calories
280

Protein
27g

Cholesterol
65mg

Total fat
9g

Saturated fat
4g

Sodium
380mg

2 litres	unsalted chicken stock	**3½ pints**	**1 tbsp**	chopped fresh mint	**1 tbsp**
4	garlic cloves, finely chopped	**4**	**1 tbsp**	fresh thyme, or **¾** tsp dried	**1 tbsp**
1	lemon, juice only	**1**		thyme	
	freshly ground black pepper		**350 g**	unpeeled aubergine, cut into	**12 oz**
4	chicken breasts, skinned and	**4**		1 cm (½ inch) cubes	
	boned (about 500 g/1 lb)		**60 g**	feta cheese, soaked 10 minutes	**2 oz**
1.25 kg	ripe tomatoes, skinned, seeded,	**3**		in cold water to remove some of	
	and coarsely chopped, or 800 g			its salt, drained and crumbled	
	(28 oz) canned tomatoes, drained				
	and chopped				

Bring the stock to the boil in a large, heavy-bottomed saucepan. Add the garlic, half of the lemon juice and a generous grinding of pepper; reduce the heat and add the chicken. Poach the chicken at a simmer until the meat feels springy to the touch – about 5 minutes.

Use a slotted spoon to remove the chicken from the poaching liquid. When the chicken is cool enough to handle, cut it into small cubes

and put the cubes in a bowl. Toss the chicken with the mint and the remaining lemon juice, and set it aside to marinate.

Add the tomatoes and thyme to the stock, and simmer the liquid for 10 minutes. Add the aubergine and cook for 5 minutes more. Stir in the chicken and its marinade and simmer the soup for 2 minutes. Serve the soup with the cheese sprinkled on top.

Chicken Soup with Chilies, Cabbage and Rice

Serves 4

Working time: about 20 minutes

Total time: about 1 hour

Calories 285

Protein 20g

Cholesterol 60mg

Total fat 11g

Saturated fat 2g

Sodium 275mg

1 tbsp	safflower oil	1 tbsp			freshly ground black pepper	
750 g	chicken thighs, skinned, fat trimmed	1¼ lb	¼ tsp	salt		¼ tsp
			90 g	long-grain rice		3 oz
1	garlic clove, finely chopped	1	2	large dried mild chili peppers, stemmed, split lengthwise and seeded		2
3	spring onions, trimmed and sliced into thin rounds	3				
¼ litre	unsalted chicken stock	16 fl oz	1	large carrot, julienned		1
1 tbsp	fresh thyme, or ¾ tsp dried thyme	1 tbsp	175 g	shredded Chinese cabbage		6 oz

Heat the safflower oil in a large, heavy-bottomed saucepan over medium-high heat. Add the chicken thighs and sauté them, turning them frequently, until they are evenly browned – 3 to 4 minutes. Push the chicken to one side of the pan; add the garlic and spring onions and cook them for 1 minute, stirring constantly. Pour in the stock and ¾ litre (1¼ pints) of water. Add the thyme and some pepper, and bring the liquid to the boil. Reduce the heat to maintain a simmer and cook the mixture, partially covered, for 20 minutes. Skim any purities from the surface and simmer the liquid for 20 minutes more.

While the stock is simmering, bring ¼ litre (8 fl oz) of water and ⅛ tsp of the salt to the boil in another pan. Add the rice and stir once, reduce the heat and cover the pan. Simmer the rice until all of the water is absorbed – about 20 minutes.

While the rice is cooking, pour ¼ litre (8 fl oz) of boiling water over the chilies and soak for 15 minutes. Purée the chilies with their liquid.

Remove the chicken thighs from the pan and set aside. When the chicken is cool enough to handle, remove the meat from the bones and cut into small pieces. Return the chicken pieces to the pan. Add the carrot, cabbage, rice and the remaining salt. Simmer and cook the soup until the carrot is tender – 3 to 4 minutes. Strain the chili purée through a fine sieve into the soup. Stir in the purée and serve at once.

Beef Soup with Brussels Sprouts and Sweet Potato

Serves 4
as a first
course

Working
time: about
30 minutes

Total time:
about
1 hour and
30 minutes

Calories
225

Protein
28g

Cholesterol
75mg

Total fat
7g

Saturated fat
3g

Sodium
190mg

500 g	beef shin bones	1 lb	150 g	sweet potato, peeled and cut	5 oz
500 g	lean beef, finely diced	1 lb		into 2 cm (¾ inch) cubes	
1	small onion, thinly sliced	1	1 tsp	finely chopped fresh rosemary,	1 tsp
1	garlic clove, finely chopped	1		or ½ tsp dried rosemary	
1	small bay leaf	1	¼ tsp	salt	¼ tsp
125 g	Brussel sprouts, trimmed and halved lengthwise	4 oz		freshly ground black pepper	

Place the shin bones, beef, onion, garlic, and bay leaf in a large, heavy-bottomed saucepan. Pour in 2.5 litres (4 pints) of water and bring it to the boil. Reduce the heat to maintain a strong simmer. Cook the mixture, partially covered, for 1 hour, occasionally skimming off the impurities that rise to the surface.

Remove and discard the bones and bay leaf. Increase the heat to high and cook the mixture until the liquid is reduced to about ¾ litre (1¼ pints) – 10 to 15 minutes. Add the Brussel sprouts, sweet potato and rosemary. Reduce the heat and simmer the soup until the vegetables are tender – 8 to 10 minutes. Stir in the salt and some pepper, and serve the soup immediately.

Pork Soup with Chinese Cabbage

<table>
<tr><td>

Serves 6

Working (and total) time: about 25 minutes

</td><td>

</td><td>

Calories
230

Protein
20g

Cholesterol
50mg

Total fat
5g

Saturated fat
1g

Sodium
300mg

</td></tr>
</table>

4 tbsp	rice wine or dry sherry	**4 tbsp**
2 tbsp	cornflour	**2 tbsp**
1 tbsp	finely chopped fresh ginger root	**1 tbsp**
500 g	pork fillet, trimmed of all fat, thinly sliced across the grain	**1 lb**
6	dried Asian mushrooms, covered with boiling water and soaked for 20 minutes, stemmed and thinly sliced, soaking liquid reserved	**6**

125 g	vermicelli or thin egg noodles	**4 oz**
¼ tsp	salt	**¼ tsp**
1.5 litres	unsalted chicken stock	**2½ pints**
3 tbsp	rice vinegar	**3 tbsp**
2 tsp	soya bean paste	**2 tsp**
250 g	Chinese cabbage, thinly sliced	**8 oz**
6 tbsp	fresh coriander leaves	**6 tbsp**
¼ tsp	dark sesame oil	**¼ tsp**

Pour the wine into a non-reactive bowl and stir in the cornflour and ginger. Add the pork and stir gently to coat it with the liquid. Set the bowl aside.

Add the vermicelli or noodles to 1 litre (1¾ pints) of boiling water with ¼ teaspoon of salt. Start testing the pasta after 3 minutes and cook it until it is *al dente*. Drain and rinse it under cold water and set it aside.

Carefully pour 12.5 cl (4 fl oz) of the mushroom-soaking liquid into a measuring jug, leaving the grit behind, then pour the measured liquid into a large, heavy-bottomed pan. Add the mushrooms, stock, vinegar and bean paste. Bring the liquid to the boil, then stir in the pork slices with their marinade and the cabbage. Return the liquid to the boil and add the vermicelli, coriander and sesame oil. Cook the soup until the pasta is heated through – about 2 minutes. Transfer the soup to a warmed bowl and serve it at once.

Turkey-Lentil Soup

Serves 6

Working time: about 15 minutes

Total time: about 1 hour

Calories 220

Protein 22g

Cholesterol 45mg

Total fat 5g

Saturated fat 1g

Sodium 185mg

750 g	turkey drumsticks, skinned	**1½ lb**
	freshly ground black pepper	
2 tsp	safflower oil	**2 tsp**
1	small onion, thinly sliced	**1**
190 g	lentils, picked over and rinsed	**7 oz**
1	small bay leaf	**1**
1	small carrot, thinly sliced	**1**

1	small courgette, thinly sliced	**1**
1	stick celery, thinly sliced	**1**
1	ripe tomato, skinned, seeded	**1**
	and coarsely chopped	
½ tsp	finely chopped fresh sage,	**½ tsp**
1	or ¼ tsp dried sage	**1**
⅜ tsp	salt	**⅜ tsp**

Sprinkle the drumsticks with some pepper. Heat the oil in a large, heavy-bottomed saucepan over medium heat. Add the drumsticks and cook them, turning them frequently, until they are evenly browned – 2 to 3 minutes. Push the drumsticks to one side of the pan, then add the onion and cook it until it is translucent – 2 to 3 minutes.

Pour 1.25 litres (2 pints) of water into the pan. Add the lentils and bay leaf, and bring the water to the boil. Reduce the heat to maintain a simmer and cook the lentils, covered, for 20 minutes. Skim off any impurities that have risen to the surface. Continue cooking the mixture until the juices run clear from a drumstick pierced with the tip of a sharp knife – about 20 minutes more.

Remove the drumsticks and set them aside. When they are cool enough to handle, slice the meat from the bones and cut it into small pieces; discard the bones. Remove and discard the bay leaf. Add the carrot, courgette, celery and tomato to the soup and simmer until the vegetables are tender – about 5 minutes. Add the turkey meat, sage and salt, and continue cooking the soup until the vegetables are tender – about 2 minutes more. Serve hot.

Lamb Broth with Winter Vegetables

1 tbsp	safflower oil	1 tbsp
1	small onion, thinly sliced, slices separated into rings	1
750 g	lamb shoulder, knuckle end, trimmed	1½ lb
4 tbsp	pearl barley	4 tbsp
1	bay leaf	1
1 tsp	chopped fresh thyme, or ¼ tsp dried thyme	1 tsp
1	garlic clove, finely chopped	1
½ tsp	salt	½ tsp
¼ tsp	crushed black peppercorns	¼ tsp
1	turnip, peeled and cut into 1 cm (½ inch) cubes	1
1	small swede, peeled and cut into 1 cm (½ inch) cubes	1
1	carrot, cut into 1 cm (½ inch) cubes	1

Heat the oil in a large, heavy-bottomed saucepan over medium heat. Add the onion rings and cook them until they are browned – about 8 minutes. Add the lamb, bay leaf, thyme, garlic, salt and crushed peppercorns. Pour in 3 litres (5¼ pints) of water and bring the liquid to the boil. Reduce the heat and simmer the mixture, partially covered, for 1¼ hours.

Remove the bay leaf and discard it. Remove the lamb joint from the pan; when the lamb is cool enough to handle, slice the meat from the bone and cut it into small cubes. Return the lamb cubes to the pan. Simmer the soup, uncovered, over medium heat until it is reduced by half – about 15 minutes. Add the turnip, swede and carrot, cover the pan, and simmer the soup until the vegetables are tender – about 15 minutes more. Serve immediately.

Vegetable Soup with Grilled Chicken

Serves 4

Working time: about 30 minutes

Total time: about 1 hour

Calories 255

Protein 16g

Cholesterol 25mg

Total fat 10g

Saturated fat 2g

Sodium 320mg

2	chicken breasts, skinned and boned (about 250 g/8 oz)	2
1 tsp	olive oil	1 tsp
1	lime, juice only	1
	freshly ground black pepper	
1	large red onion, chopped	1
1.5 litres	unsalted chicken stock	2½ pints
500 g	ripe plum tomatoes, skinned, seeded and chopped, or 400 g (14 oz) canned tomatoes, drained and chopped	1 lb
⅛ tsp	ground coriander	⅛ tsp
¼ tsp	cayenne pepper	⅛ tsp
¼ tsp	ground cumin	¼ tsp
½ tsp	dried oregano	½ tsp
1	carrot, julienned	1
1	courgette, julienned	1
125 g	water chestnuts, julienned	4 oz
1 tbsp	finely cut chives	1 tbsp
2	garlic cloves, finely chopped	2
	Tortilla-Strip Garnish	
3	corn tortillas	3
1 tbsp	olive oil	1 tbsp

Cut each breast horizontally into two thin, flat pieces. Set them on a large plate, dribble the tsp of oil and the lime juice over them and sprinkle with some pepper. Let the chicken marinate while you make the rest of the soup.

Combine the onion, garlic and stock in a pan over medium-high heat. Boil the stock, add the tomatoes, coriander, cayenne pepper, cumin, oregano and salt. Simmer the mixture for 20 minutes. Add the carrot, courgette and chestnuts,

and simmer until tender – about 6 minutes.

Just before the vegetables are done, preheat the grill. Remove the chicken from the marinade, cook until firm to the touch – about 2 minutes on each side. Cut on the diagonal into thin slices.

Brush the tortillas with the tbsp of olive oil and cut them into thin strips. Spread the strips out on a baking sheet and grill until crisp.

Arrange the chicken on the soup and sprinkle with chives. Serve the tortilla strips separately.

Turkey Goulash Soup

Serves 6 as a first course

Working time: about 30 minutes

Total time: about 45 minutes

Calories 260
Protein 24g
Cholesterol 40mg
Total fat 6g
Saturated fat 1g
Sodium 290mg

2 tsp	safflower oil	**2 tsp**	
500 g	onions, thinly sliced	**1 lb**	
2	sweet green peppers, seeded, deribbed and cut into 2 cm (¾ inch) squares	**2**	
2 tbsp	paprika, preferably Hungarian	**2 tbsp**	
¼ tsp	ground cumin	**¼ tsp**	
	freshly ground black pepper		

2 litres	unsalted chicken stock	**3½ pints**	
2 tbsp	cornflour	**2 tbsp**	
125 g	wide egg noodles	**4 oz**	
500 g	turkey escalopes, sliced across the grain into 5 cm (2 inch) long strips	**1 lb**	
⅜ tsp	salt	**⅜ tsp**	

Heat the safflower oil in a large, heavy-bottomed saucepan over medium heat. Add the sliced onions and cook them until they are browned – about 15 minutes. Stir in the green peppers, paprika, cumin, some black pepper and all except 4 tablespoons of the stock. Combine the cornflour and the reserved stock, and add this mixture to the pan. Simmer the stock, partially covered, for 20 minutes.

While the stock is simmering, add the noodles to 2 litres (3½ pints) of boiling water with ½ teaspoon of salt. Start testing the noodles after 5 minutes and cook them until they are *al dente*. Drain the noodles, rinse them under cold running water, and set them aside.

Add the turkey strips to the simmering stock and poach them until they are opaque – 3 to 4 minutes. Stir in the noodles and the ⅜ teaspoon of salt. Cook the soup for 2 minutes more; serve at once.

Onion and Red Potato Soup with Walnut Toasts

Serves 4
as a first
course

Working
(and total)
time: about
30 minutes

Calories
220

Protein
7g

Cholesterol
2mg

Total fat
9g

Saturated fat
1g

Sodium
290mg

1 litre	unsalted chicken stock	**1¾ pints**
2	onions (about 300 g/10 oz) cut into eighths	**2**
250 g	red-skinned potatoes, unpeeled, cut into 2 cm (¾ inch) pieces	**8 oz**
2		**2**
¼ tsp	salt	**¼ tsp**
	freshly ground black pepper	

4	garlic cloves, finely chopped	**4**
4 tbsp	coarsely chopped walnuts, plus 4 large walnut halves	**4 tbsp**
4	slices of French bread, each about 5 mm (¼ inch) thick	**4**
4 tbsp	thinly sliced fresh basil leaves	**4 tbsp**

Pour the stock into a large saucepan over medium heat. When the stock begins to steam, add the onions, potatoes, salt, some pepper and half of the garlic. Simmer the liquid until the potatoes can be easily pierced with a fork – 10 to 15 minutes.

While the potatoes are cooking, preheat the oven to 200°C (400°F or Mark 6). Using a mortar and pestle, crush 3 tablespoons of the walnuts with the remaining garlic to form a paste. Spread one quarter of the paste on each slice of bread,

then press a walnut half into the centre of each slice. Toast the bread in the oven until the slices are slightly browned on the bottom – about 5 minutes.

Stir the basil into the soup and immediately ladle the soup into four heated bowls. Float a walnut-covered slice of bread in the centre of each bowl; sprinkle some of the remaining chopped walnuts around each slice and serve the soup immediately.

Beef and Wild Mushroom Soup

Serves 8

Working time: about 50 minutes

Total time: about 1 hour

Calories 185

Protein 17g

Cholesterol 40mg

Total fat 8g

Saturated fat 2g

Sodium 375mg

10	dried shiitake or Asian black mushrooms, covered with ½ litre (16 fl oz) of boiling water and soaked for 20 minutes	10
1.5 litres	unsalted chicken stock	2½ pints
2 tbsp	safflower oil	2 tbsp
500 g	rump steak, trimmed of fat and cut into 1 cm (½ inch) wide strips	1 lb
5	garlic cloves, finely chopped	5
2	onions, finely chopped	2

125 g	fresh shiitake or field mushrooms, stems trimmed, thinly sliced	4 oz
250 g	button mushrooms, stems trimmed, thinly sliced	8 oz
½ tsp	salt	½ tsp
12.5 cl	Madeira, dry sherry or Marsala	4 fl oz
	freshly ground black pepper	
2 tbsp	low-sodium soy sauce or shoyu	2 tbsp
2 tbsp	chopped fresh parsley, preferably flat-leaf	2 tbsp

Remove the soaked mushrooms from their liquid; reserve the liquid. Cut off and discard the stems. Thinly slice the caps and set them aside. Slowly pour all but about 12.5 cl (4 fl oz) of the mushroom-soaking liquid into a large pan, leaving the grit behind; discard the gritty liquid. Add the stock to the pan and bring to a simmer.

While the liquid is heating, pour 1 tablespoon of the oil into a large, heavy frying pan over medium-high heat. When the oil is hot, add the beef and sauté it, stirring constantly, for 2 minutes. Remove the beef and set it aside.

Pour the remaining oil into the frying pan. Add the chopped garlic and onion and sauté them for 30 seconds, stirring constantly. Stir in all of the soaked and fresh mushrooms and ¼ tsp of the salt. Sauté, stirring frequently, for 5 minutes. Pour in the Madeira, sherry or Marsala and stir to scrape up and dissolve any caramelized bits. Add the contents of the frying pan to the stock with the remaining salt, some pepper and the soy sauce. Simmer for 20 minutes.

Stir in the sautéed beef strips and cook for 1 minute more. Serve garnished with the parsley.

Cream of Chicken Soup

Serves 6

Working time: about 20 minutes

Total time: about 2 hours

Calories 240

Protein 34g

Cholesterol 105mg

Total fat 10g

Saturated fat 5g

Sodium 160mg

1.5 kg	chicken	**3 lb**
1.5 litres	unsalted vegetable stock	**2¼ pints**
1	bay leaf	**1**
2	blades of mace	**2**
1	small bunch of parsley	**1**
½ tsp	salt	**½ tsp**
15 g	unsalted butter, softened	**½ oz**
15 g	flour	**½ oz**
3 tbsp	double cream	**3 tbsp**
	freshly ground black pepper	
	chopped parsley for garnish	

Wipe the chicken well with paper towels and place it in a large saucepan with the stock, bay leaf, mace, parsley and salt. Bring the liquid to the boil over medium heat, skim the scum from the surface, then reduce the heat to low. Cover the pan and cook the chicken gently for 1 hour.

Strain the stock through a fine sieve into a large jug. Cool the stock rapidly by standing the jug in iced or very cold water for about 30 minutes. When the fat has congealed, remove it from the surface of the cooled stock.

Meanwhile, remove and discard the skin and bones from the chicken. Cut the flesh into small pieces.

Put the chicken pieces and cooled stock into a blender or food processor and purée until very smooth. Return the soup to the saucepan.

Blend the butter and flour together to make a smooth paste. Heat the soup almost to the boil, then gradually whisk in the butter and the flour. Bring to the boil, stirring all the time, then reduce the heat and simmer the soup for 10 minutes. Stir in the cream and season with pepper. Serve garnished with parsley.

Oyster Soup with Leeks

Serves 6

Working (and total) time: about 45 minutes

Calories
125
Protein
8g
Cholesterol
50mg
Total fat
5g
Saturated fat
3g
Sodium
115mg

15 g	unsalted butter	**½ oz**
2	large leeks, trimmed, split, washed thoroughly to remove all grit and thinly sliced	**2**
2 tsp	fresh thyme, or ½ tsp dried thyme	**2 tsp**
3	garlic cloves, finely chopped	**3**

12.5 cl	dry white wine	**4 fl oz**
60 cl	fish stock	**1 pint**
⅛ tsp	salt	**⅛ tsp**
	freshly ground black pepper	
250 g	freshly shucked large oysters	**8 oz**
4 tbsp	single cream	**4 tbsp**

Melt the butter in a large, heavy-bottomed saucepan over medium-high heat. Add the leeks and thyme, then cover the pan and cook the leeks, stirring them several times, for 10 minutes

Add the garlic and wine; continue cooking, stirring frequently, until the wine evaporates – about 5 minutes. Pour in the stock, then add the salt and some pepper, and simmer the mixture for 10 minutes.

While the stock is simmering, set aside 12 of the oysters. Purée the remaining oysters with their liquid in a food processor or blender.

Remove the pan from the heat, then whisk in the oyster purée and the cream. Set the pan over very low heat and cook the soup just long enough to heat it through – about 3 minutes. Place two of the reserved oysters in each of six heated soup plates. Pour the soup over the oysters and serve at once.

Crab, Fennel and Tomato Soup

Serves 4

Working time: about 45 minutes

Total time: about 2 hours

Calories 120

Protein 13g

Cholesterol 60mg

Total fat 4g

Saturated fat 1g

Sodium 380mg

2 tbsp	virgin olive oil	2 tbsp
1	onion, thinly sliced	1
1	small fennel bulb, trimmed, cored and thinly sliced, several stems and leaves reserved for the stock and for garnish	1
3	garlic cloves, finely chopped	3
500 g	ripe tomatoes, skinned, seeded and chopped, or 400 g (14 oz) canned tomatoes, drained and chopped	1 lb

½ tsp	salt	½ tsp
	cayenne pepper	
250 g	white crab meat	8 oz
	Fish Stock	
500 g	lean fish bones and trimmings	1 lb
1	large onion, thinly sliced	1
1	stick celery, thinly sliced	1
	several parsley stems (optional)	
½ litre	dry white wine	16 fl oz
8–10	peppercorns	8–10

To make the stock, pour 1.5 litres (2½ pints) of water into a large pan and add the fish bones and trimmings, onions, celery, reserved fennel stems and a few fennel leaves, parsley if using. Boil, then simmer for 15 mins, skimming off any foam. Add the wine and return to boil. Simmer for 10 mins; add peppercorns and simmer 5 mins more.

Strain stock into a bowl and discard solids. Return to the pan and boil until reduced to about 1 litre (1¾ pints).

Heat the oil in another large pan over medium-low heat. Add the onion, fennel and garlic. Cover the pan and cook the vegetables, stirring, until they are soft – 10 to 15 minutes. Stir in the tomatoes, salt and a pinch of cayenne pepper. Pour in the reduced stock and bring to the boil. Reduce heat and simmer, covered, until the fennel is very soft – about 45 minutes.

Purée the fennel-tomato mixture in batches in a blender/processor until it is very smooth. Return the purée to the pan and add the crab meat. Cook the soup over medium-low heat until warm; garnish with remaining fennel leaves.

Haddock and Sweet Pepper Soup

Serves 4

Working time: about 25 minutes

Total time: about 1 hour

Calories 125

Protein 20g

Cholesterol 75mg

Total fat 3g

Saturated fat 1g

Sodium 135mg

500 g	haddock fillets, skinned, rinsed, patted dry, and cut into 2.5 cm (1 inch) cubes	**1 lb**
2 tbsp	finely chopped fresh ginger root	**2 tbsp**
2 tbsp	dry sherry	**2 tbsp**
1.5 litre	fish stock	**2½ pints**
4	garlic cloves, thinly sliced	**4**

¼ tsp	salt	**¼ tsp**
⅛ tsp	cayenne pepper	**⅛ tsp**
1	sweet red pepper, skinned, seeded, deribbed and cut into narrow strips about 2.5 cm (1 inch) long	**1**
1	sweet yellow pepper, skinned, seeded, deribbed and cut into narrow strips about 2.5 cm (1 inch) long	**1**

Place the fish cubes in a shallow dish. Scatter the ginger over them and pour in the sherry. Marinate the fish at room temperature for 30 minutes.

Meanwhile, pour the fish stock into a large, shallow pan and bring it to the boil. Stir in the sliced garlic, salt and cayenne pepper, and reduce the heat to maintain a strong simmer. Cook the mixture with the cover ajar for 30 minutes.

Add the pepper strips to the pan and cook them for 3 minutes. Pour the marinade into the pan and reduce the heat to maintain a gentle simmer. Add the fish and cook it gently until it is opaque and feels firm to the touch – about 3 minutes. Serve the hot soup immediately.

Editor's Note: To remove the skins from the sweet peppers, grill them on all sides until the skins blister and blacken. Cover with a damp cloth, or put them in a bowl and cover with plastic film, and leave to cool; then peel off the skins.

Oyster Soup with Watercress and Carrot

Serves 4			
Working time: about 40 minutes			
Total time: about 1 hour			

Calories
245

Protein
14g

Cholesterol
70mg

Total fat
8g

Saturated fat
2g

Sodium
365mg

1 tbsp	safflower oil	1 tbsp		cayenne pepper	
1	onion, finely chopped	1	¼ tsp	white pepper	¼ tsp
125 g	celeriac, peeled and finely chopped	4 oz	1	large carrot, julienned	1
1	potato, peeled and finely chopped	1	250 g	shucked oysters, liquid reserved	8 oz
12.5 cl	dry white wine	4 fl oz	90 g	watercress leaves	3 oz
35 cl	fish stock	12 fl oz	2 tsp	finely cut chives (optional)	2 tsp
¼ litre	semi-skimmed milk	8 fl oz	1 tsp	paprika, preferably Hungarian (optional)	1 tsp

Heat the oil in a large, heavy-bottomed saucepan over medium-high heat. Add the onion and celeriac and cook them until the onion is translucent – 4 to 5 minutes. Add the potato, wine and stock, then reduce the heat and simmer the mixture, covered, until the vegetables are quite soft – 15 to 20 minutes. Purée the mixture in a blender or food processor and return it to the pan. Stir in the milk along with a pinch of cayenne pepper, the white pepper and salt.

Blanch the julienned carrot in ½ litre (16 fl oz) of boiling water for 2 to 3 minutes. Remove the

pieces with a slotted spoon and stir them into the soup.

Put the oysters and their liquid in a small saucepan over medium heat. Gently simmer the oysters until they begin to curl at the edges – 3 to 4 minutes. Transfer the oysters and their liquid to the soup; bring the soup to a simmer (do not let it boil) and add the watercress. Simmer the soup until the watercress is wilted – 2 to 3 minutes. Sprinkle the chives and paprika over the top, if you are using them, and serve the soup immediately.

Clam and Rice Soup

Serves 4

Working time: about 35 minutes

Total time: about 50 minutes

Calories 140

Protein 7g

Cholesterol 25mg

Total fat 4g

Saturated fat 1g

Sodium 40mg

24	small hardshell clams, scrubbed	24
1 tbsp	virgin olive oil	1 tbsp
90 g	onion, finely chopped	3 oz
2 tsp	finely chopped garlic	2 tsp
1	small bay leaf	1
45 g	long-grain rice	1½ oz

4 tbsp	dry white wine	4 tbsp
⅛ tsp	crushed saffron threads	⅛ tsp
½ tsp	fresh lemon juice	½ tsp
1	large, ripe tomato, skinned, seeded and finely chopped	1
2 tbsp	finely chopped fresh parsley	2 tbsp

Bring 1 litre (1¾ pints) of water to the boil in a large pan. Add the clams, cover the pan tightly, and cook the clams until they open – about 5 minutes. Transfer the clams to a plate, discarding any that remain closed, and reserve the cooking liquid. When the clams are cool enough to handle, remove them from their shells. Discard the shells and set the clams aside.

Heat the oil in a heavy frying pan over medium heat. Add the onion, garlic and bay leaf, and sauté them, stirring frequently, until the onion is translucent – about 5 minutes.

Strain the clam-cooking liquid through a sieve lined with muslin, then pour the liquid back into the pan. Add the contents of the frying pan along with the rice, wine, saffron and lemon juice, and bring to the boil. Reduce the heat and cover the pan, leaving the lid ajar; simmer for 10 minutes, stirring once or twice. Add the tomato and simmer for 5 minutes more. Stir in the parsley and cook for 2 minutes longer. Return the clams to the pan and heat them through. Serve immediately.

Spinach and Fish Soup

Serves 6

Working
time: about
25 minutes

Total time:
about
1 hour

Calories
125

Protein
17g

Cholesterol
7mg

Total fat
3g

Saturated fat
1g

Sodium
215mg

2	onions, sliced	2
2	sticks celery, sliced	2
¼ tsp	ground mace	¼ tsp
½ tsp	fresh thyme, or ⅛ tsp dried thyme	½ tsp
1	bay leaf	1
	freshly ground black pepper	
1.25 litres	fish stock or unsalted chicken stock	2 pints
500 g	fillet from a firm, white-fleshed fish, such as haddock or coley, skinned and cut into 2.5 cm (1 inch) chunks	1 lb
2 tbsp	farina	2 tbsp
750 g	spinach, stemmed and washed	1½ lb
2 tbsp	double cream	2 tbsp

Put the onions, celery, mace, thyme, bay leaf and some pepper into a large pan. Pour in ¼ litre (8 fl oz) of the stock and bring to the boil. Cover the pan, reduce the heat to maintain a strong simmer, and cook the vegetables and seasonings for 30 minutes. Remove the lid and increase the heat to medium high. Cook until the liquid has evaporated and the onions are lightly browned.

Meanwhile, pour the remaining stock into a large shallow pan over medium-high heat and bring it to a simmer. Add the fish chunks and poach them in the simmering stock until they are opaque and feel firm to the touch – about 3 minutes. Remove the fish pieces and set them aside; reserve the poaching liquid.

Transfer ¼ litre (8 fl oz) of the poaching liquid to a small saucepan and boil. Whisk in the farina and cook the liquid until it thickens – about 4 minutes. Set the liquid aside.

Pour the remaining poaching liquid into the pan containing the vegetables. Stir in the spinach and cook over medium-high heat until it wilts – about 4 mins. Purée the spinach mixture with the farina-liquid in 2 batches in a blender/food processor. Return the soup to the pan over medium heat. Stir in the cream and the fish, and cook the soup for 2 mins. Serve immediately.

Shanghai Scallop Soup with 20 Garlic Cloves

Serves 4

Working (and total) time: about 40 minutes

Calories
230
Protein
25g
Cholesterol
45mg
Total fat
3g
Saturated fat
1g
Sodium
355mg

500 g	scallops, bright white connective tissue removed, large scallops halved or quartered	1 lb	250 g	bok choy, leaves cut into chiffonade, stems sliced into 5 mm (¼ inch) pieces	8 oz
2 tbsp	dry sherry	2 tbsp	4 tbsp	fresh lemon juice	4 tbsp
1 tbsp	low-sodium soy sauce or shoyu	1 tbsp	60 g	cellophane noodles, soaked in hot water for 20 minutes, drained and cut into 2.5 cm (1 inch) lengths	2 oz
	freshly ground black pepper				
1.5 litres	unsalted chicken stock	2½ pints			
20	garlic cloves, peeled	20	1 tbsp	chopped fresh coriander	1 tbsp

Rinse the scallops under cold water and drain. Put them into a bowl with the sherry, soy sauce and some pepper. Gently stir the scallops to coat them with the marinade; set aside.

Pour the stock into a large pan and bring it to the boil. Add the garlic cloves, reduce the heat and simmer until the cloves are tender – about 15 minutes. Then stir in the bok choy leaves and

stems, and simmer for 5 minutes more. Stir in the lemon juice, noodles and scallops with their marinade. Cook until the scallops are opaque – about 1 minute. Stir in the coriander and serve.

Editor's Note: If bok choy (also called Chinese chard) is not available, Swiss chard can be substituted.

Chilled Tomato and Prawn Soup

Serves 4		
Working time: about 20 minutes		
Total time: about 1 hour and 20 minutes (includes chilling)		

Calories 120		
Protein 14g		
Cholesterol 95mg		
Total fat 1g		
Saturated fat 0g		
Sodium 150mg		

½ litre	unsalted veal or chicken stock	**16 fl oz**	**¼ tsp**	white pepper	**¼ tsp**
4	tomatoes, skinned, seeded, chopped	**4**	**1 tsp**	Dijon mustard	**1 tsp**
½	cucumber, peeled, seeded, chopped	**½**	**4–8**	drops Tabasco sauce	**4–8**
1	spring onion, trimmed and sliced	**1**	**350 g**	cooked peeled prawns or shrimps	**12 oz**
2 tbsp	red wine vinegar	**2 tbsp**		croûtons (optional)	

Pour the stock into a serving bowl. Stir in the tomatoes, cucumber, spring onion, vinegar, pepper, mustard and Tabasco sauce. Add the prawns and stir again. Cover the bowl and refrigerate it for at least 1 hour. Serve the soup in chilled soup bowls; if you wish, garnish each portion with a few croûtons.

Hot and Sweet Soup with Seafood Dumplings

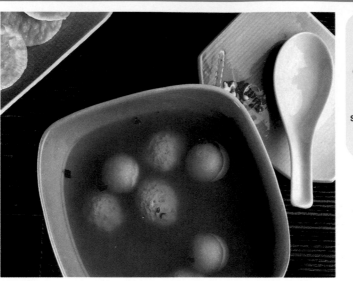

Serves 8

Working
time: about
1 hour

Total time:
about
1 hour and
15 minutes

Calories
135

Protein
17g

Cholesterol
75mg

Total fat
3g

Saturated fat
1g

Sodium
240mg

250 g	finely chopped lean pork	**8 oz**
250 g	fresh prawns, peeled, deveined	**8 oz**
	if necessary, and finely chopped	
250 g	white crab meat, picked over	**8 oz**
2	spring onions, trimmed and finely	**2**
	chopped	
1½ tsp	finely chopped fresh ginger root	**1½ tsp**
1	egg white, beaten	**1**

2 litres	unsalted chicken stock	**3½ pints**
2 tsp	sweet chili sauce, or 1 tsp	**2 tsp**
	crushed hot red pepper flakes	
	mixed with 2 tsp golden syrup	
	and 1 tsp vinegar	
12.5 cl	fresh lemon juice	**4 fl oz**
250 g	small cantaloupe melon balls	**8 oz**
¼ tsp	salt	**¼ tsp**

Combine the pork, prawns, crab meat, spring onions, ginger and egg white in a large bowl. Shape heaped teaspoonfuls of the mixture into dumplings about 2.5 cm (1 inch) in diameter, moistening your palms from time to time to keep the mixture from sticking to them.

Pour the stock into a large pan and bring it to the boil. Reduce the heat to maintain a strong simmer and add the chili sauce or pepper-flake mixture and 4 tablespoons of the lemon juice.

Gently drop half of the dumplings into the hot liquid and simmer them for 5 minutes. Remove the dumplings with a slotted spoon and set them aside. Drop the remaining dumplings into the liquid and simmer them for 5 minutes. When the second batch is done, return the first batch of dumplings to the pan. Heat the dumplings through, then add the melon balls, the salt and the remaining lemon juice. Serve the soup in individual bowls.

Fish Soup with Red Pepper Sauce

Serves 6

Working (and total) time: about 45 minutes

Calories
205

Protein
17g

Cholesterol
35mg

Total fat
9g

Saturated fat
1g

Sodium
160mg

1.5 litres	fish stock	**2½ pints**
3	large leeks, green tops discarded, white parts split, washed thoroughly to remove all grit, and thinly sliced	**3**
250 g	finely shredded Savoy cabbage	**8 oz**
2	ripe tomatoes, skinned, seeded and chopped	**2**
500 g	fillet from a firm, white-fleshed fish such as cod, rinsed and cut into 2.5 cm (1 inch) chunks	**1 lb**

4 tbsp	freshly grated pecorino cheese	**4 tbsp**
	Red Pepper Sauce	
2	wholemeal bread slices, crusts removed	**2**
1	sweet red pepper, seeded, deribbed and chopped	**1**
2	large garlic cloves, chopped	**2**
⅛ tsp	cayenne pepper	**⅛ tsp**
3 tbsp	virgin olive oil	**3 tbsp**

To prepare the red pepper sauce, first put the bread slices into a bowl and pour in enough water to cover them. Soak the slices for 10 minutes, then squeeze out the water and transfer the bread to a food processor. Add the red pepper, garlic and cayenne pepper, and purée the mixture. With the machine still running, dribble in the olive oil; the resulting sauce should be thick. Set the sauce aside.

For the soup, pour the stock into a large pan and bring it to the boil. Add the leeks, cabbage and tomatoes, then reduce the heat and simmer the vegetables until they are tender – about 10 minutes. Add the fish and cook the soup until the fish is firm and opaque – about 3 minutes. Pass the cheese and the red pepper sauce in separate bowls.

Sweetcorn, Scallop and Fettuccine Soup

Serves 4 Working (and total) time: about 25 minutes	

Calories
330

Protein
21g

Cholesterol
45mg

Total fat
9g

Saturated fat
3g

Sodium
385mg

350 g	scallops, bright white connective tissue removed, large scallops cut in half horizontally	**12 oz**	**175 g**	frozen sweetcorn kernels	**6 oz**
⅛ tsp	white pepper	**⅛ tsp**	**1 tbsp**	safflower oil	**1 tbsp**
½ tsp	salt	**½ tsp**	**15 g**	unsalted butter	**½ oz**
¼ litre	semi-skimmed milk	**8 fl oz**	**2 tbsp**	finely chopped shallots	**2 tbsp**
1 litre	fish stock	**1¾ pints**	**12.5 cl**	dry white wine	**4 fl oz**
125 g	spinach fettuccine	**4 oz**	**½ tsp**	chopped fresh thyme, or ⅛ tsp dried thyme	**½ tsp**

Rinse the scallops under cold running water and drain them. Season the scallops with the pepper and ¼ teaspoon of the salt, and set them aside.

Pour the milk and stock into a large pan. Sprinkle in the remaining salt and bring the liquid to the boil. Add the fettuccine and sweetcorn. Cover the pan until the liquid returns to the boil, then cook until the pasta is *al dente* – about 8 minutes.

While the fettuccine and sweetcorn are cooking, heat the oil and butter together in a heavy frying pan over medium-high heat. Add the scallops and sauté them for 30 seconds on each side. Add the shallot and cook, stirring, for 1 minute. Pour in the wine, then add the thyme and cook for 1 minute more.

When the pasta is ready, combine it with the scallop mixture and serve at once.

A Fine Kettle of Fish

Serves 8

Working (and total) time: about 45 minutes

Calories
200

Protein
25g

Cholesterol
95mg

Total fat
6g

Saturated fat
1g

Sodium
190mg

1.5 litres	fish stock or unsalted chicken stock	**2½ pints**
¼ litre	dry white wine	**8 fl oz**
2 tbsp	virgin olive oil	**2 tbsp**
4	spring onions, trimmed and finely chopped	**4**
16	small hardshell clams, scrubbed	**16**
16	mussels, scrubbed and debearded	**16**
750 g	redfish (or Norway haddock) fillets, cut into 2.5 cm (1 inch) cubes	**1½ lb**
16	fresh prawns, peeled, deveined if necessary	**16**

750 g	ripe tomatoes, skinned, seeded and coarsely chopped, or 400 g (14 oz) canned tomatoes, drained and coarsely chopped	**1½ lb**
3 tbsp	finely cut chives	**3 tbsp**
1	lemon, grated rind only	**1**
⅛ tsp	cayenne pepper	**⅛ tsp**
⅛ tsp	crushed saffron seeds	**⅛ tsp**
4 tbsp	finely chopped fresh parsley	**4 tbsp**
1 tbsp	fresh thyme, or ¾ tsp dried thyme	**1 tbsp**

Put stock, wine, oil and spring onions in a pan and bring to boil. Add the clams and mussels and cook them, partially covered, for 2 mins. Remove the opened shellfish and set them aside. Partially cover the pan again and cook for 2 mins more. Remove the opened shellfish; discard any that remain closed. Strain the cooking liquid into a bowl through a sieve lined with muslin. Rinse the pan and return the liquid to it.

Add the prawns and fish to the pan and return the liquid to the boil. Stir in the tomatoes, chives, thyme, lemon rind, cayenne pepper, saffron and parsley. Add the reserved clams and mussels and remove the pan from the heat. Let the soup stand for 5 minutes so that the flavours may meld.

Divide the clams, mussels and prawns between eight bowls. Ladle some fish and broth into each, and serve.

Vietnamese Crab and Asparagus Soup

Serves 6

Working (and total) time: about 30 minutes

Calories
130
Protein
16g
Cholesterol
60mg
Total fat
5g
Saturated fat
1g
Sodium
390mg

4	dried Asian mushrooms, covered with ¼ litre (8 fl oz) of boiling water and soaked for 20 minutes	4
1 tbsp	safflower oil	1 tbsp
3	spring onions, trimmed, the white parts chopped, the green tops thinly sliced crosswise	3
3	garlic cloves, finely chopped	3
1.25 litres	unsalted chicken stock	2 pints
250 g	fresh asparagus, trimmed and cut diagonally into 2.5 cm (1 inch) pieces	8 oz
1 tbsp	fish sauce or low-sodium soy sauce	1 tbsp
	freshly ground black pepper	
500 g	white crab meat, picked over	1 lb
2 tbsp	chopped fresh coriander, plus several whole leaves for garnish	2 tbsp

Strain the mushroom-soaking liquid through a fine sieve lined with muslin and set the liquid aside. Cut off and discard the stems; slice the caps.

Heat the oil in a heavy pan over medium-high heat. Add the white spring onion parts and the garlic; sauté them, stirring often, for 1 minute. Pour in the mushroom-soaking liquid and the stock, then add the mushroom caps and bring the mixture to the boil. Add the asparagus, the fish sauce or soy sauce, the green spring onion tops and some pepper. Return the liquid to the boil, then reduce the heat to maintain a simmer. Cook the asparagus pieces until they are barely tender – about 3 minutes.

Add the crab meat and stir in the chopped coriander. Simmer the soup for 2 minutes more to heat the crab through. Garnish the soup with the coriander leaves before serving.

Gingery Pear Soup

Serves 4
as a first
course

Working
time: about
10 minutes

Total time:
about
30 minutes

Calories
150

Protein
4g

Cholesterol
6mg

Total fat
6g

Saturated fat
1g

Sodium
210mg

1 tbsp	safflower oil	1 tbsp	½ litre	unsalted chicken stock	16 fl oz
2 tbsp	finely chopped fresh ginger root	2 tbsp	¼ tsp	salt	¼ tsp
			¼ litre	semi-skimmed milk	8 fl oz
1 tbsp	finely chopped shallot	1 tbsp	4	parsley sprigs for garnish	4
4 tbsp	pear brandy (optional)	4 tbsp			
500 g	pears, quartered, cored and sliced into thin wedges	1 lb			

Heat the oil in a large, heavy-bottomed saucepan over medium heat. Add the ginger and shallot and cook them, stirring, until the shallot is translucent – 2 to 3 minutes. Pour in the brandy if you are using it, and cook the mixture until the liquid is nearly evaporated – about 3 minutes more.

Add the pears, stock and salt. Reduce the heat and simmer the mixture, partially covered, until the pears are translucent and soft – 15 to 20 minutes. Remove a few pear slices and set them aside for garnish.

Purée the contents of the pan in a food processor or blender. Return the purée to the pan, stir in the milk and warm the soup over low heat, taking care that it does not boil. Serve the soup immediately, garnished with the reserved pear slices and the parsley sprigs.

Golden Gazpacho

Serves 6
as a first
course

Working
time: about
15 minutes

Total time:
about
1 hour and
15 minutes
(includes
chilling)

Calories
75
Protein
3g
Cholesterol
1mg
Total fat
1g
Saturated fat
0g
Sodium
20mg

1	ripe melon, peeled, seeded and diced	1
2	garlic cloves, peeled	2
2	sweet yellow peppers, seeded, deribbed and quartered	2
½–1	hot green chili pepper, seeded and deribbed	½–1
30 g	fresh coriander leaves	1 oz

1	orange, peeled and quartered, rind of one quarter reserved	1
35 cl	fresh orange juice	12 fl oz
3	spring onions, white parts only	3
1½ tbsp	fresh lime juice	1½ tbsp
12.5 cl	plain low-fat yogurt	4 fl oz
12	fresh coriander leaves for garnish	12

Place all the ingredients except the yogurt in a food processor and purée the mixture. Add the yogurt and operate the machine in short bursts until the yogurt is mixed in. Transfer the soup to a bowl or jar, cover it tightly, and refrigerate it for at least 1 hour.

Garnish each serving with the coriander leaves.

Editor's Note: In the event that sweet yellow peppers cannot be found, use sweet red peppers instead.

Peach Soup Flambé

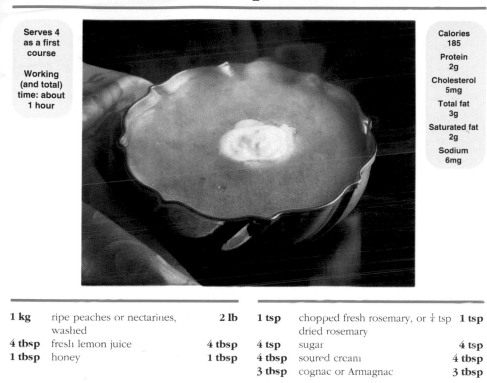

Serves 4
as a first
course

Working
(and total)
time: about
1 hour

Calories
185

Protein
2g

Cholesterol
5mg

Total fat
3g

Saturated fat
2g

Sodium
6mg

1 kg	ripe peaches or nectarines, washed	**2 lb**	**1 tsp**	chopped fresh rosemary, or $\frac{1}{4}$ tsp dried rosemary	**1 tsp**
4 tbsp	fresh lemon juice	**4 tbsp**	**4 tsp**	sugar	**4 tsp**
1 tbsp	honey	**1 tbsp**	**4 tbsp**	soured cream	**4 tbsp**
			3 tbsp	cognac or Armagnac	**3 tbsp**

Pour 2 litres (3½ pints) of water into a large pan. Bring the water to the boil, then add the peaches and cook them until their skins loosen – 5 to 15 minutes, depending on their ripeness. Using a slotted spoon, remove the peaches and set them aside to cool. Pour off all but 35 cl (12 fl oz) of the cooking water.

When the peaches are cool enough to handle, peel them, then cut them in half and remove the stones. Discard the skins and stones; return the peach halves to the pan. Add the lemon juice, honey, rosemary and 3 teaspoons of the sugar and bring the mixture to the boil. Reduce the heat and simmer the peaches, stirring frequently,

for 15 minutes.

Purée the mixture in batches in a blender, a food processor or a food mill. Pour the purée back into the pan and reheat it slowly over low heat, stirring occasionally, for about 10 minutes. Stir in 2 tablespoons of the soured cream.

Transfer the soup to a warmed serving bowl. Mix the remaining soured cream with the remaining sugar, then spoon the mixture on to the centre of the soup. Gently spoon the cognac or Armagnac round the soured cream, taking care that the brandy floats on the surface of the soup. Dim the lights, ignite the brandy, and serve the soup with the flames dancing.

Useful weights and measures

Weight Equivalents

Avoirdupois		Metric
1 ounce	=	28.35 grams
1 pound	=	254.6 grams
2.3 pounds	=	1 kilogram

Liquid Measurements

$1/4$ pint	=	$1 1/2$ decilitres
$1/2$ pint	=	$1/4$ litre
scant 1 pint	=	$1/2$ litre
$1 3/4$ pints	=	1 litre
1 gallon	=	4.5 litres

Liquid Measures

1 pint	= 20 fl oz	= 32 tablespoons
$1/2$ pint	= 10 fl oz	= 16 tablespoons
$1/4$ pint	= 5 fl oz	= 8 tablespoons
$1/8$ pint	= $2 1/2$ fl oz	= 4 tablespoons
$1/16$ pint	= $1 1/4$ fl oz	= 2 tablespoons

Solid Measures

1 oz almonds, ground = $3 3/4$ level tablespoons
1 oz breadcrumbs fresh = 7 level tablespoons
1 oz butter, lard = 2 level tablespoons
1 oz cheese, grated = $3 1/2$ level tablespoons
1 oz cocoa = $2 3/4$ level tablespoons
1 oz desiccated coconut = $4 1/2$ tablespoons
1 oz cornflour = $2 1/2$ tablespoons
1 oz custard powder = $2 1/2$ tablespoons
1 oz curry powder and spices = 5 tablespoons
1 oz flour = 2 level tablespoons
1 oz rice, uncooked = $1 1/2$ tablespoons
1 oz sugar, caster and granulated = 2 tablespoons
1 oz icing sugar = $2 1/2$ tablespoons
1 oz yeast, granulated = 1 level tablespoon

American Measures

16 fl oz	=1 American pint
8 fl oz	=1 American standard cup
0.50 fl oz	=1 American tablespoon

(*slightly smaller than British Standards Institute tablespoon*)

0.16 fl oz	=1 American teaspoon

Australian Cup Measures

(*Using the 8-liquid-ounce cup measure*)

1 cup flour	4 oz
1 cup sugar (crystal or caster)	8 oz
1 cup icing sugar (free from lumps)	5 oz
1 cup shortening (butter, margarine)	8 oz
1 cup brown sugar (lightly packed)	4 oz
1 cup soft breadcrumbs	2 oz
1 cup dry breadcrumbs	3 oz
1 cup rice (uncooked)	6 oz
1 cup rice (cooked)	5 oz
1 cup mixed fruit	4 oz
1 cup grated cheese	4 oz
1 cup nuts (chopped)	4 oz
1 cup coconut	$2 1/2$ oz

Australian Spoon Measures

	level tablespoon
1 oz flour	2
1 oz sugar	$1 1/2$
1 oz icing sugar	2
1 oz shortening	1
1 oz honey	1
1 oz gelatine	2
1 oz cocoa	3
1 oz cornflour	$2 1/2$
1 oz custard powder	$2 1/2$

Australian Liquid Measures

(*Using 8-liquid-ounce cup*)

1 cup liquid	8 oz
$2 1/2$ cups liquid	20 oz (1 pint)
2 tablespoons liquid	1 oz
1 gill liquid	5 oz ($1/4$ pint)